THE TRANSFORMING
WORD

THE TRANSFORMING
WORD

Discovering the Power and Provision of the Bible

Tony Evans

MOODY PUBLISHERS
CHICAGO

ISBN 0-8024-6817-9

Printed in the United States of America

*This book is gratefully dedicated to
the staff and Board of Directors of
The Urban Alternative,
who enable me to spread
God's transforming Word worldwide.*

CONTENTS

PART TWO
THE COMMUNICATION OF GOD'S WORD

PART THREE
THE BENEFITS OF GOD'S WORD

WITH GRATITUDE

Once again I want to thank my friend and editor, Philip Rawley, as we complete our seventeenth book together. My appreciation also goes out to Greg Thornton, Cheryl Dunlop, and the rest of the team at Moody Publishers for their encouragement and quality work on this project.

INTRODUCTION

My oldest grandchild's name is Kariss. When Kariss spent a night with me and her grandmother each week, it was my joyful task to take her out for doughnuts the next morning—although I went under strict orders not to buy any of those sugary angels for myself, since I didn't need the extra calories.

When we arrived at the doughnut shop, I would help Kariss decide what kind of doughnuts she wanted, taking care to recommend several kinds that looked good to me. I did this knowing full well that Kariss would never be able to eat the additional doughnuts.

And without fail, she would look at me and say, "Poppy, I can't eat all of this. Would you finish it for me?" With a smile on my face and my taste buds salivating, I happily agreed to finish her doughnut. After all, we wanted to teach our grandchildren not to waste food! My ingenious plan allowed me to eat doughnuts without actually purchasing them for myself.

The problem with my eating those doughnuts was that although they tasted good, they didn't provide me with any long-term nutritional value. The same is true today for Christians who are trading substance for succulence in their neglect of God's Word. We have become satisfied with the nonnutritious substitutes of religion, human philosophy, and other man-made ideologies at the expense of the powerful, transforming truth of Scripture.

For too many people, the Bible has become like the Queen of England. It may hold a high position, but it has no real authority. The Bible may be a great showpiece under their arms, or on their desks or coffee tables, but the truth is that it occupies a very insignificant and unproductive place in their lives.

How else can we explain the lack of power, victory, peace, testimony, and impact of God's people today despite an unprecedented flood of Christian music, Bible studies, books, programs, and conferences? There is a massive disconnect between the power of God's inerrant Word and the powerlessness of God's people.

This disconnect exists because Christians have become so secularized in our worldview that the Bible has been reduced to nothing more than a great work of spiritual inspiration instead of the authoritative Word of God. Increasingly, professing Christians are responding to opinion polls, popular human philosophies, concepts, and gimmicks to address the needs in their lives, demonstrating a lack of confidence in the sufficiency and authority of Scripture. More and more people are turning to Bible "supplements" to fix the emotional, relational, psychological, financial, and spiritual issues they face. The Bible's influence has also diminished because many pastors have stopped preaching it in its power and authority. Most preaching makes reference to the Bible, but often it is so mixed with human wisdom and opinions that it loses its divine authority and uniqueness. Thus, like a doughnut, the preaching may go down sweet because it is coated in sugar, but it has little real benefit.

This book was written to call us back from the spiritual famine now engulfing us—a famine of the Word of God (Amos 8:11).

Because we are not feeding on the Word, our malnutrition is obvious to the watching world, if not to ourselves.

But there is hope, because God's Word has lost none of its power or ability to feed us on pure spiritual truth. We must understand this unique Book so we can experience God's powerful reality in our lives, both personally and collectively. It is my unwavering conviction that there are two answers to every question: God's answer, and everybody else's answer—and everybody else is wrong. God has spoken clearly, and He has done so only through the Bible.

It is my prayer that by the time you have completed this book, your love for and desire to know the Bible will be rekindled, and you will experience the transforming work of God's transforming Word in your life.

PART
①

THE NATURE OF GOD'S WORD

1
THE
BIBLE
IS
UNIQUE

An old story is told of two men who became lost in the forest. When night fell they realized the danger they were in and began frantically looking for the way home.

As the men moved through the dark, frightening woods, they suddenly spotted a light in the distance and made their way toward it. The light was shining from an old cabin, but as one of the men approached the cabin and peeked in the window, he drew back in fear. The cabin belonged to a huge man who was well known in that region for being an eccentric hermit. Many scary stories had been told about him over the years, although no one knew for sure if he was really dangerous.

The man looking in the window quickly crawled back to his friend, being careful to stay hidden.

"What's the matter?" his friend asked.

"It's that hermit," the first man replied. "There's no way I'm going to knock on his door!" So the two men huddled in the dark woods.

After about an hour, they were so hungry and cold they realized they couldn't just stay in the forest all night. So they decided to take a risk and ask the hermit for shelter. But before they knocked they decided to have another look in the window, just to see what he was doing.

The second man volunteered this time, and he snuck up to peek in the window. He stared for a few seconds, then came running back to the other guy with a big smile of relief on his face.

"It's OK!" he said excitedly. "He's reading his Bible!"

There is no other book on earth that can turn fear into joy and doubt into assurance the way the Bible can. The Bible stands apart from and is unique among all other books and so-called sacred writings, because it alone is the very Word of God with the power to transform individual lives and entire cultures. One of the great statements the Bible makes about itself is found in Isaiah 55:

> For as the rain and the snow come down from heaven, and do not return there without watering the earth and making it bear and sprout, and furnishing seed to the sower and bread to the eater; so will My word be which goes forth from My mouth; it will not return to Me empty, without accomplishing what I desire, and without succeeding in the matter for which I sent it. (vv. 10–11)

You will never find an unconditional guarantee like this in any other piece of writing—especially a guarantee that is still good some 2,600 years after it was first made. In fact, you will never find another book that can compete with the Bible in any form or fashion whatsoever. It is without question the *transforming* Word of God.

The Bible's uniqueness may be comforting to you and me, but the world has never been quite sure what to do with the Word. Some simply try to ignore it, but that's as impossible as trying to ignore a lion in your living room. Some people put the Bible alongside the great works of philosophy that human beings have written, or categorize it as a book of wise sayings and moral lessons. To still others the Bible is a book of guidance and principles for life—and it is all of these things, but also far more. We could never exhaust the subject of the Bible's uniqueness, but I want to begin by considering several things that set the Word of God apart.

THE BIBLE IS UNIQUE IN ITS ORIGIN

Everything we are going to talk about in this book hinges on the fact that the Bible came from God. Scripture is unique because it is not the word of man, but of God.

Now some people will challenge this claim because they say their book is the Word of God. Mormons make that claim for the *Book of Mormon,* and other cults say the same about their founders' writings. And of course, Muslims make a similar claim for the Qur'an (we'll have more to say about this later).

The problem is that anyone can step forward and claim that he or she has received a revelation from God. So how do we know which claim to believe? Thankfully, we don't have to guess, because there are stringent tests that any writing must meet to be validated as the true Word of God. Since the Bible claims to be the unique revelation of God, its words must stand out from all other words. It must be self-authenticating and superior to all other books. We will see how completely the Bible stands up to these tests and validates its claim to be unique.

Jesus Testified to the Bible's Uniqueness

The most important proof of the Bible's uniqueness is Jesus' testimony to the Scriptures. The main reason we know the Bible is God's Word is that Jesus said so. He used the word *Scriptures* on a number of occasions to describe the Old Testament writings, whether the Law or the prophets (see, for example, Matthew 21:42; 22:29; 26:56).

Jesus also made a statement in the Sermon on the Mount that no one can ignore. "Truly I say to you, until heaven and earth pass away, not the smallest letter or stroke shall pass from the Law until all is accomplished" (Matthew 5:18).

When we want to emphasize a statement we often say, "Now mark my words." Jesus said that when it comes to the Bible, we can mark not only the words as true, but also every letter and even the smallest portions of the letters. In other words, the Bible is binding, authoritative, and dependable.

One implication of this is that to reject the Bible is to reject Jesus and accuse Him of being a liar. Many people who want to claim Jesus don't want to accept the Bible as His Word. But Jesus ruled out that option when He tied His life and ministry completely to the fulfillment of Scripture. Jesus used the strongest language possible to declare that the Bible is God's Word.

A Muslim once told me, "I don't believe your holy book, but I believe Jesus was a great prophet."

"OK, let's discuss that," I said. "How great a prophet was Jesus?"

"Oh, he was a great prophet just like Mohammed."

Then I asked him, "Could Jesus be a great prophet on a par with Mohammed, and yet be a persistent liar?" My Muslim friend agreed that Jesus could not be a persistent liar and a great prophet at the same time.

Then I pointed out to him the inconsistency of Islam's view of Jesus. "But that's the position you have to take if you say you believe Jesus was a true prophet and yet reject the Bible, because Jesus affirmed again and again that the Bible is God's Word. Even your holy book, the Qur'an, records Jesus as saying that the Bible is God's Word. My holy book doesn't say that Jesus ever affirmed the Qur'an as God's Word. So was Jesus lying when He said the Bible is true and will be fulfilled down to the smallest stroke of its letters?"

You see, we don't have to be afraid to assert the uniqueness of Scripture, because everything Jesus said and did proved the Bible to be true.

The Bible Testifies to Its Own Uniqueness

It would take another book to deal with all of the Scripture references where the Bible either explicitly or implicitly refers to itself as God's Word. Of course, when we say the Bible speaks of itself as God's Word, we are talking about the testimony of the authors of Scripture who recorded God's revelation.

For example, hundreds of times in the Old Testament the prophets said "the word of the Lord" came to them. Many other times God spoke directly through the patriarchs or the prophets to His people, who never failed to acknowledge that it was God who spoke.

One great statement of God's uniqueness is found in Isaiah 43, where the Lord said: "Before Me there was no God formed, and there will be none after Me. I, even I, am the Lord, and there is no savior besides Me" (vv. 10–11). If God is unique among all so-called gods, then His Word is unique.

A classic argument for the Bible's validity is the way that the Word so naturally and continually, without the slightest self-consciousness or apology, refers to itself as the Word of God. This factor has to be taken into account, for if it were otherwise and the Bible was constantly trying to defend itself or insist that it was true, we would have reason to doubt its claims—much like a judge and jury might begin to doubt a witness who kept loudly insisting that he was telling the truth.

Another proof of the Bible's uniqueness is the very nature of the truths it teaches. What I mean here is that the Bible gives unmistakable evidence that its thoughts come from God and not man. We began this chapter by looking at Isaiah 55:10–11. Now I want to consider verses 8–9, which also make a strong case for the Bible's uniqueness: "'For My thoughts are not your thoughts, nor are your ways My ways,' declares the Lord. 'For as the heavens are higher than the earth, so are My ways higher than your ways and My thoughts than your thoughts.'"

That's a very strong claim, so if the Bible is indeed unique, then its thinking should be so far higher than our thinking that we could never figure it out on our own. And that is exactly the case with

Scripture. This argument may not satisfy the skeptics, but the fact is that the doctrines of Scripture, such as man's total ruin in sin and helplessness to save himself, and the incarnation of God Himself to save mankind, are utterly apart from any other religious teachings. Someone has said that the Bible is the only book that has the courage to tell us the truth about ourselves.

Clearly, the Bible did not originate with men. The apostle Peter gave us the definitive word on God's revelation. "But know this first of all, that no prophecy of Scripture is a matter of one's own interpretation, for no prophecy was ever made by an act of human will, but men moved by the Holy Spirit spoke from God" (2 Peter 1:20–21). No author ever wrote a word of Scripture until the Holy Spirit moved him to write.

The Bible's Perfect Unity Testifies to Its Uniqueness

The Bible is also unique in the way it has come down to us. The Bible's unity of message is nothing short of a miracle, given that it was written over a period of about fifteen hundred years by forty or more different people, who lived in several different countries with different cultures and came from every kind of background imaginable.

Just try bringing together a liberator and national leader (Moses), a military general (Joshua), two kings (David and Solomon), a shepherd (Amos), a tax collector (Matthew), some fishermen (Peter and John), and a rabbi (Paul), have them write down even the simplest message, and see if they can agree with each other. That wouldn't happen even if they were in the same room at the same time working with the same set of facts, let alone separated by hundreds of years.

The thin red line of our Redeemer and His blood runs all the way through the Bible—from the first prophecy of a Savior and God's slaying of animals to cover Adam and Eve (Genesis 3:15, 21), to the last chapter of Revelation that invites the redeemed to spend eternity with God (Revelation 22:17). The Bible's message is consistent and unified from beginning to end. I love the psalmist's statement: "The sum of Your word is truth" (Psalm 119:160).

Now don't let anyone intimidate you on this one. Someone will say, "Yeah, but the Bible is full of contradictions." That's an old charge that has never been demonstrated, and those who make it usually can't point to one example. Let me tell you, the world has had about two thousand years to prove this charge, and yet the Bible still stands. The best answer to this charge is to hand the skeptic a Bible and ask him to show you an example of a contradiction. Most people have no idea what to do because they're just repeating a line they've heard.

In the 1970s a mechanic came forward after the death of billionaire Howard Hughes, claiming that Hughes had made him his heir because the man had once rescued Hughes when he found him staggering around in the desert. The mechanic supposedly had Hughes's true will, naming him as heir.

This mechanic's story had all kinds of holes in it, and it didn't take skeptical officials very long to expose his claim as bogus. We're talking about one man's story that didn't even depend on anyone else's validation, and yet he couldn't make it work. But even though the Bible has been examined, dissected, and attacked by the greatest minds in history, no one has ever made a charge of inconsistency or contradiction stick against God's Word. You can relax, too, because it is never going to happen. No one but God could make one perfectly unified document out of sixty-six books. The unity of the Bible is like that of the human body, in which every part can only be explained in reference to the whole (see Psalm 119:160a).

Now someone might say, "You're just using circular reasoning here. You're going to the Bible to authenticate the Bible." OK, then let's turn to other sources outside of the Scripture to help verify its truth and corroborate the Bible's witness to itself.

History Testifies to the Bible's Uniqueness

When I make this argument I am not talking about the Bible as a supernatural document, but as a work of historical literature. The point here is that if people accepted the same standards of validity for the Bible that they readily accept for other historical documents, they would have to admit that the Bible is the most widely attested book ever written.

To show you what I mean, we can take any figure from history who is no longer on the scene. How do we know that George Washington was our nation's first president? Nobody alive today can say, "I have seen George Washington. I've met him and heard him speak, and I know he was real." We accept the historicity of George Washington because we trust the historical record we have about him. And the same can be said for many other people we could name from history.

One test of the validity of any historical record is its proximity to the life of the person whose history it records. One reason the history of George Washington is considered reliable is that much of it was written during his lifetime by people who did see and know him, and more of it was written in the years very soon after his death. The closer the historical record is to the person's life, the more valid it becomes.

Well, guess what? The Bible comes through with shining colors on this score. The very latest part of the New Testament, the book of Revelation, was written in the 90s A.D., about sixty years after Jesus' death. But it was also written by the apostle John, an eyewitness to Jesus' life, so that gives his writings added weight.

This is amazing testimony to the Bible's trustworthiness. By comparison, some of the famous writings of antiquity, such as those that tell of people like Julius Caesar, were recorded hundreds of years after the events they describe. Many critics attack the early dates for various books of the New Testament, because they know that if they admit the Gospels and Epistles were written so soon after Jesus' life and death—mostly by eyewitnesses—their case against the Bible is greatly weakened.

Another test of the Bible's historical validity is the number of existing manuscripts that corroborate it. We are told that ten copies exist of the account of Julius Caesar crossing the Rubicon, one of the most famous events of ancient history. The earliest of these manuscripts was written hundreds of years after the event, yet the fact of Caesar's crossing has never been seriously questioned by historians.

But the Bible puts that record, and almost any other historical record, to shame. We have about five thousand copies of the New Testament in existence, from fragments of a single verse to entire books. These copies agree on the basic doctrines of the faith and the important facts of Jesus' life, although there are many differences of words and the order of events. This record is unheard of in historical circles, yet the Bible continues to come under attack.

But I can say it again. Fear not the doubts of the skeptics, for in God's Word we have an authentic historical record. The Bible runs into trouble with its critics because of its supernatural, convicting character, not because it is of doubtful authenticity.

THE BIBLE IS UNIQUE IN ITS TEACHING

A book that is unique in its origin should also be unique in its content and what it teaches. The Bible qualifies on this point because it teaches what no other book does. The Bible claims to teach the whole truth and nothing but the truth about God, man, creation, sin, salvation, and any other subject it touches on. Let's consider some of the Bible's unique truths.

Only the Bible Teaches About the Trinity

Other religious books may teach that there is a God, but only the Bible teaches that God is a triune Being. God's Word is unique in affirming that God is "one in three"—three distinct Persons who share the same divine essence (see Matthew 28:19).

If the doctrine of the Trinity sometimes keeps you up at night trying to figure it out and explain it, join the crowd. Theologians have been trying to do that for centuries, and yet the truth of the Trinity remains a mystery. Other religions reject it, and Muslims use it to claim that Christians are the "infidels," or unbelievers, because they say we are polytheists who worship various gods, while they are the true monotheists who worship only Allah.

But the mystery of the Trinity does not negate the fact that God has revealed Himself to us as Father, Son, and Holy Spirit. I liken the Trinity to a pretzel, which has three holes that are distinct yet completely intertwined and interconnected, all sharing the same piece of dough.

We know the Persons of the Godhead are distinct because of statements like this by Jesus: "My Father is working until now, and I Myself am working" (John 5:17). Jesus also promised that God would send the Holy Spirit after Jesus' resurrection (John 14:26). But at the same time Jesus also said, "I and the Father are one" (John 10:30). Three yet one is the glory and the mystery of the Trinity, and only the Bible teaches it.

Only the Bible Teaches the Whole Truth About Jesus

Jesus testified to the truth of Scripture, and the Scripture also testifies to the truth about Jesus. The Bible's teaching of Christ's virgin birth, sinless life as perfect Man and eternal God in a human body, atoning death, and triumphant resurrection are enough to set this Book apart from all others.

The Bible presents Jesus as the God-man, totally unlike anyone else in history. One minute He was hungry because He was man, but the next minute He was creating enough food to feed five thousand people because He is God. He slept because He was tired, yet He also raised people from the dead. He died on the cross because He was man, yet He walked out of the grave because He is God. The guards who were sent to arrest Jesus one time came back so awed that all they could say was, "Never has a man spoken the way this man speaks" (John 7:46).

Mohammed said he was a prophet whose job was to point people to Allah, the god of Islam. But Jesus said, "I am the true God." Not only that, but He received worship that only belongs to God. The apostle Thomas confessed after Jesus had answered his doubts,

"My Lord and my God!" (John 20:28). Far from rebuking or correcting Thomas, Jesus pronounced as blessed those who believe in Him without seeing Him (v. 29).

Philip said to Jesus at the Last Supper, "Lord, show us the Father, and it is enough for us" (John 14:8). Jesus answered with a statement of His equality with God: "Have I been so long with you, and yet you have not come to know Me, Philip? He who has seen Me has seen the Father" (v. 9).

Perhaps the most startling claim Jesus made to His deity is when He said to the Jews one day, "Before Abraham was born, I am" (John 8:58). That blew their minds, because they understood that Jesus was claiming to be the pre-existent God, the One who appeared to Moses in the burning bush and called Himself, "I AM WHO I AM" (Exodus 3:14). The whole truth about Jesus is that He is the God-man, and the Bible alone teaches that.

Only the Bible Teaches the Whole Truth About Man

The Bible's teaching about the origin and nature of mankind also sets it totally apart. Other religious writings have their stories and myths about how the human race began, but the Bible is alone in portraying man as not only the unique creation of God, but as utterly ruined by sin and completely helpless even to improve himself, to say nothing of saving himself, apart from God's intervention.

Because it is the revealed truth of God, the Bible explains and probes the depth of human nature in a way no other book does. The testimony of countless people is that even though they thought they were reading the Bible, they realized that the Bible was reading them. This is so because the Bible is alive. Hebrews 4:12 says that God's Word is "living and active and sharper than any two-edged sword, and piercing as far as the division of soul and spirit, of both joints and marrow, and able to judge the thoughts and intentions of the heart."

You cannot get any deeper into a person's life than to divide between the soul and spirit, the immaterial part of man. The Bible tells us our deepest needs, and explains why nothing or no one can meet those needs except God.

We are creatures of dust, and yet the Bible says we breathe the very breath of God. We are deeply flawed by sin, and our nature is depraved—which means that on our own we are incapable of doing anything good that would commend us to God. The world is surprised when a sinner sins because the world doesn't believe that human beings are sinners by nature and by choice. You won't find that truth anywhere but in the Bible.

Only the Bible Teaches the Whole Truth About Salvation

Here's another unique characteristic of Scripture. Every other religion known to mankind tells you what you must do to make yourself acceptable to God. But the Bible tells you what God has already done to save you.

There are really only two religions in the world—the kind in which you do your best to reach up to God, and the kind in which He gave His best to reach down to you. Unlike any other religious book, the Bible says we are saved by grace and not by works (see Ephesians 2:8–9).

Even though I know that men's hearts are sinful and they don't want God, it still amazes me at times that people would reject God's free offer of salvation. Everything that needs to be done to save us has been done. Most people want to do something to try to save themselves, but the Bible has no loopholes a person can squeeze through to make it into heaven apart from the blood of Jesus Christ.

Only the Bible Teaches History in Advance

Teaching history in advance sounds like an oxymoron—and it would be for any book but the Bible. God's Word teaches about history hundreds of years before it happens, which is called prophecy. If we had no other validation of Scripture but its fulfilled prophecies, we would still be on very solid ground.

There have been many so-called prophets in history, and some of them seemed to make some accurate prophecies. But the Bible's standard is 100 percent accuracy, whether the prophecy is one hundred or five hundred years in advance of its fulfillment. It's not even worth discussing other prophets' records, because no prophet in any holy book has ever claimed to prophesy the future on the scale of the Bible.

One of the Bible's most amazing prophecies to me is one of its most familiar: the prophecy that Jesus Christ would be born in the village of Bethlehem. This prophecy was given in Micah 5:2, which was written about seven hundred years before Christ's birth. Its fulfillment is recorded in Matthew 2:5–6.

The time frame of this alone is miraculous, but it's even more so when you consider that Bethlehem is just a dot on the map. In other words, the chances of prophesying Jesus' birth and getting it right by accident are zero.

And don't forget that biblical prophecy isn't limited to religious events. The book of Daniel contains the progression of the Gentile world powers in the centuries before Christ, written hundreds of years before Alexander the Great and the Greeks defeated the Medo-Persian Empire and then were in turn defeated by the Romans. You can close your Bible and open your history book, and you'll find that God tells the story of world history in advance—because the Bible is unique in its teaching.

THE BIBLE IS UNIQUE IN ITS IMPACT

We are going to consider two more ways in which the Bible demonstrates that it is unique, and then I want to ask you an important question before we go on to the next chapter.

In some ways we have already made the point that the Bible has had, and continues to have, an influence that is unequaled by any book in history. My point here is simply to reinforce the incredible impact that God's Word has made on the world. God promises in Isaiah 55:11 that His Word will always accomplish the purpose for which He sends it. That is obvious from the influence the Bible has in this world.

The Bible Has Changed Millions of Individuals

When I was a student at Dallas Seminary, we used to hear a story that was told about the late Dr. Harry Ironside, who was one of the great Bible teachers in the early half of the twentieth century and a frequent lecturer at the seminary.

The story goes that Dr. Ironside was preaching in a town once when a local atheist challenged him to prove the existence of God and tried to argue that atheism was as beneficial a way of life as Christianity.

Dr. Ironside challenged the man to a contest. "I want you to find one hundred people whose lives have been changed and made better by atheism, and I will find one hundred people whose lives have been radically changed by the gospel of Jesus Christ. We'll meet here tomorrow, and see which way is the true way." Needless to say, the man couldn't meet the challenge, because only the Bible has life-changing power.

The Bible Has Changed Entire Cultures

The Bible has also changed entire cultures. I love the story of the unbelieving anthropologist who visited a primitive tribe that had accepted the gospel, seeking evidence against Christianity. The chief told the scientist that he knew Christianity was true. When his visitor asked the chief how he knew that, he replied, "Because if it weren't, we would eat you."

Closer to home, William Wilberforce was an Englishman who was elected to Parliament in 1780. He served there for many years, and in the course of time he became convinced from reading his Bible that slavery was wrong. He learned of the evils of slavery in the British Empire and launched a long and exhausting struggle to end the practice. Slavery was eventually outlawed, and Wilberforce is credited with being the main force behind the change. And he was changed by reading his Bible and allowing the Holy Spirit to convict his heart.

The United States is far from perfect, but perhaps more than any other nation, many of our laws and ideas were intentionally based on the teachings of God's Word. And even though our nation has strayed far from God, His Word still has a deep impact on our culture and ways of thinking.

The Bible has also influenced and changed cultures in areas such as science and literature, a legacy we can still see today even though the secular world is working hard to erode its influence. But nothing will change or bring down God's Word.

THE BIBLE IS UNIQUE IN ITS PRESERVATION

Someone has said that although a blacksmith's anvil may take many blows from the hammer, the anvil stands firm while the hammers break. The Bible is an anvil that has shattered the hammers of many who have tried to destroy it.

The Bible is also unique in its preservation. It has survived for several thousand years, even though kings and the world's mightiest powers and intellects have been trying to destroy it for centuries.

Think about it. How many books have not only survived for several thousand years, but are still being read, debated, and sold around the world today? I can only name one. Bible societies tell us that when they go into a country where Bibles are scarce, people stand in line for hours and even days to receive a copy. Chinese university students pass around any portion of the Bible they can get their hands on and memorize all they can. Would to God that American college students would start doing this!

No book in history has been preserved like the Bible. Why wouldn't it be, if God is the author? He is going to take care of His Book. Nations have outlawed the Bible, tried to destroy every copy, and killed people for translating and printing it. People like William

Tyndale and John Wycliffe are among the heroes of the faith who dedicated their lives to making sure we have the Bible in our hands.

The Bible records an amazing story in Jeremiah 36, an attempt made by King Jehoiakim of Judah to destroy God's message that the prophet Jeremiah had recorded on a scroll. The king cut up the scroll and burned it (vv. 22–23), but God simply told Jeremiah to get another scroll and write His Word on it again.

The eighteenth-century French philosopher Voltaire despised the Christian church and boasted that within fifty years of his death, Christianity would be extinct and people would have to go to a museum to see a Bible. Yet after Voltaire died, his house was acquired by the French Bible Society and used to print and distribute Bibles.

God says His Word will stand forever (see Psalm 119:89; Isaiah 40:8). "Heaven and earth will pass away, but My words will not pass away," Jesus declared (Matthew 24:35). There is no destroying the Bible, because it is the eternal Word of God.

IS THE BIBLE UNIQUE TO YOU?

That may seem like an unusual question, but I'm not asking if you believe that the Bible is the true Word of God. I pray that you do—or, if not, that you will by the time you finish reading this book.

My question has to do with the fact that so many of the people who say with their lips that they believe the Bible is the one and only Word of God don't say it with their lives. That is, they don't allow the Word to shape their lives, and the way we know this is by the large number of Christians and church people who go to every other source but the Word for the solution to their needs and problems.

You see, what we really believe in our heads always shows up in our feet. If the Bible is the last place we go for help, we can't expect God to get excited about helping us. If our attitude is that we only go to the Bible when all else has failed, we may go years without getting things right.

This is why the Bible seems to have no life or power for so many of us. We read it, but find it unhelpful or even boring. Voltaire was dead wrong about the Bible being only a museum piece, but many Christians treat it that way when they display it on their shelves or coffee tables, but don't live by it.

But let me tell you, when the Word of God gets down into your heart, you will be different! When you understand that the Bible is the very breath and mind and heart of God on paper, then you'll discover it's alive. And you'll understand why Jesus said, "Man shall not live on bread alone, but on every word that proceeds out of the mouth of God" (Matthew 4:4).

2
THE BIBLE IS TRUTH

A college professor stood up before his class one day and said, "I want to begin this philosophy class by getting to the bottom line with a statement that will govern everything we study and talk about this semester. The bottom line of this philosophy class is that there are no absolutes. There is no such thing as absolute truth, no propositions that are true in every circumstance. Let me say it again. The bottom line of this philosophy class is that there are no absolutes."

A student in the back raised his hand and said, "Professor, may I ask a question?"

"Yes."

"You said there is no such thing as absolutes, and no such thing as a statement of absolute truth. Are you absolutely sure about that? Because if you are, you have just given us a statement of an absolute that is true in every circumstance, which is a contradiction of the assertion you just made that there are no absolutes."

That exchange may sound like the kind of academic double-talk that makes parents wonder what in the world their children are learning in college and why they have to pay so much for it. But the student who challenged his professor made a very important and valid point about the issue of truth, and about the absurdity and contradictions people get themselves into when they try to deny the existence of a concept called truth. I don't know what grade that student got in his philosophy class, but he deserved an A.

You see, that professor would have been a lot more honest with himself and his students if he had said, "Look, I have a personal bias when it comes to philosophy that you need to know about, because it is going to govern everything I present to you this semester. In fact, I'm going to try to persuade you to accept my bias as your own. My bias is against the concept of absolute truth, which to me is an outmoded relic from our religious past that needs to be discarded.

"Now I realize that I can't demonstrate to you with perfect certainty that truth does not exist, but truth is not part of my personal worldview because I don't want to be governed by any absolute standard, or answer to any Being who claims to have absolute truth. This is my bias and belief, and I am going to proceed on that basis in this class. If you believe differently, it's because you are still afflicted with your parents' outmoded mind-set or some kind of religious training."

This is what the professor was really saying; he just didn't want to admit it. Plus, it's a lot easier and takes less breath to announce, "There is no such thing as absolute truth." But I want you to see that this is actually a statement of faith as surely as when you and I say we believe that Jesus Christ is the Savior of the world. The problem with a professor's bias is that it has a ring of authority and finality to it because of his status, and the students often buy into his views.

THE INESCAPABLE ISSUE OF TRUTH

How would you react to a doctor who was unsure of his diagnosis of your condition, but gave you a prescription anyway, which you

• •

took to a pharmacist who wasn't even sure he was giving you the medicine the doctor had hesitantly prescribed? You would probably run for your life from both of them, since your health and life might be at stake! You want to go to a doctor and pharmacist who believe in truth, a fixed standard of reality that guides their decisions.

The problem is that many people who insist on living by truth in the physical realm confidently reject it in the spiritual realm. But simply announcing that truth does not exist does not solve anything. We are faced with this thing called truth, and we have to do something with it.

Pontius Pilate asked the question of the ages when truth Incarnate in the Person of Jesus Christ stood before him on trial. Jesus said to Pilate, "For this I have been born, and for this I have come into the world, to testify to the truth. Everyone who is of the truth hears My voice" (John 18:37).

Pilate responded, "What is truth?" (v. 38).

If that evil Roman governor had been an honest seeker, he would have found the answer to his question. In fact, Jesus had definitively answered Pilate's question the night before at the Last Supper, during His prayer to the Father on our behalf: "Sanctify them in the truth; Your word is truth" (John 17:17). The Bible is truth—the whole truth and nothing but the truth.

Looking for Truth in All the Wrong Places

There may have been a day when affirming among ourselves as Christians that the Bible is true would have been enough, and we could close this chapter and go on to the next one. But if that simpler day ever existed, it doesn't anymore. Not only is the world today more confused about truth than ever, but the church is confused too. That's why we need to talk about the implications of Jesus' statement that the Bible is truth.

The world has always been confused and divided on the question of truth. There have been a myriad responses to the question, "What is truth?" We have just talked about the denier, for the lack of a better term. This is the person who simply dismisses and rejects the very concept of truth.

The agnostic says that absolute knowledge on issues such as God's existence cannot be attained in this life. Since the word *agnostic* literally means "without knowledge," the agnostic's answer to Pilate's question would be "I don't know." This person is supposedly the perpetual questioner and seeker after truth—although in reality, many people who claim to be agnostics aren't working very hard to search out the truth. They are content to say that truth can't be known and leave it at that.

The rationalist says that human reason and experience are the ultimate criteria for determining truth. Rationalism focuses on the mind and simply says that whatever the mind conceives of as being reality is, in fact, truth. Rationalism thus limits the search for truth. It is one of the theories that came into play during the eighteenth-century movement known as the Enlightenment when the truths upon which Christianity is based came under sustained attack and were largely abandoned.

When I was in college, we learned about a school of thought called positivism, which said truth is limited to that which can be validated by the scientific method. If science authenticates a theory, then perhaps we can regard it as truth. Positivism doesn't leave any room for a supernatural Savior with a supernatural revelation, because these things cannot be reduced to the scientific method of testing something and repeating it time and again in the lab until its reality can be established.

Another of mankind's many answers to the question of truth is fideism, which reacted to the rationalistic and scientific method by saying that truth is subjective and personal. Truth is what we feel at the moment to be true, so therefore what's true for me may not be true for you.

Pragmatism is yet another means of seeking to arrive at truth. Pragmatism appeals to a lot of people because it says that truth is whatever works. This kind of approach is tailor-made for our

American love of "common sense" thinking that looks at a problem and wants to produce solutions.

I need to mention one other significant route people have taken to try and arrive at truth. This is man-made religion, defined as humanity's best attempts to reach up to and understand God—or even deny that He exists or cares about what happens to us. The religionist may be the hardest person of all to deal with, because he's the guy who claims to be a follower of God and a seeker after spiritual truth. But more often than not, religion begins by denying the absolute truth that God has spoken with finality in Jesus Christ (see Hebrews 1:1–2).

Beginning at the Beginning

All of these approaches may have elements of truth to them, but they are all inadequate in and of themselves as means of arriving at what the late Christian philosopher Francis Schaeffer used to call "true truth," which is the truth about God and His Word. The problem is that even though the world's greatest minds have been taking these routes and hitting dead ends for thousands of years, multimillions of people still continue to follow them, because, as we said earlier, people don't want to be held accountable to a God who will judge them by an absolute, unswerving standard.

As you can see from our brief list, the problem is not that people refuse to search for truth. They just refuse to begin with the real Source of truth. Jesus said to those who opposed Him and His message, "You search the Scriptures because you think that in them you have eternal life; it is these that testify about Me; and you are unwilling to come to Me so that you may have life" (John 5:39–40). Paul also spoke of people who are "always learning and never able to come to the knowledge of the truth" (2 Timothy 3:7).

The proliferation of television and radio talk shows is one example of what the Bible talks about when it says people are always looking and never finding. Former *Tonight* show host Johnny Carson once joked there were so many talk shows popping up that producers were going through the telephone book to get hosts. "So if your name hasn't come up yet," Carson said, "just be patient. You'll get your chance."

Although there are some informative programs on the air, the average show features all manner of guests who offer their opinions—and everybody has an opinion. And now viewers and listeners can call and weigh in with their views. But rather than being a discussion of truth, these shows are often babble by the hour. So if the issue of truth is inescapable, we need to ask what the nature of truth is and what the Bible has to say about man's endless quest for something that is real.

THE NATURE OF TRUTH

It's interesting to read a dictionary definition of truth. You probably haven't done that in a long time, so let me give you a few of the terms you might encounter. One source says that truth is "actuality," "fact," a "transcendent fundamental or spiritual reality."

Terms like these suggest an informal definition of truth that most people on the street would agree with. That is, truth is that which conforms to reality, the way things actually are. Truth is an accurate statement of the facts. My generation grew up with Sergeant Joe Friday of the television program *Dragnet,* whose famous statement was, "The facts, ma'am, just the facts." The opposite of truth in this definition is falsehood, and the opposite of telling the truth is lying.

Now the academic world may be debating and debunking the whole idea of truth, but the Bible clearly distinguishes that which is actual and genuine from that which is false. To say that something is true or false only makes sense if those two realities exist.

The Bible says clearly that truth not only exists, but that it is knowable if we truly desire to know it. Both halves of this claim may have been normative in our grandparents' day, but they sound radical in today's increasingly truth-less world. Jesus said in John 8:32, "You will know the truth, and the truth will make you free." Jesus said that truth was not only knowable, but powerful since it is the door to true freedom.

Notice that the Lord strengthened His statement by putting the definite article "the" in front of "truth." This tells us that for Jesus, truth was a definite body of material or reality. We are seeking to establish in this chapter that this body of truth which is "the truth" is the Bible.

There Are Many Claims to Truth Today

Now if you're tracking with me, you may already see the problem that our culture has with truth today. The man on the street may not disagree with you that there is such a thing as truth, but he may passionately believe that there is no such thing as truth that is the same for every person in every place and time. More than likely, he will tell you that there are many kinds of truth that are different for everyone. In other words, truth is whatever is right for you.

As I write these words, our culture is in the middle of a fierce debate over the issue of same-sex marriages and the push by homosexuals for full recognition. I have a feeling this issue will be as relevant when you read this book as it is while I'm writing it.

When people are debating issues like homosexuality, we often hear this question raised: Whose truth are we going to accept? Those who believe the Bible say that this activity is sin, while the psychological profession has now removed homosexuality from its list of disorders. Christians hold to the Bible as revealed truth from God, but as far as the world is concerned the Bible is just one voice among many in the marketplace claiming to present the truth.

I am not saying that people cannot discover certain truths on their own. But the problem with the world's "truth" is that it often has to be revised or discarded when new facts are uncovered. Hundreds of years ago, people were convinced the earth was flat. It was feared that if explorers sailed to the edge of the earth, they might fall off. But that "truth" had to be discarded as new evidence was found.

How about a contemporary example of changing truth? If you

follow the world of nutrition and health today, your head is probably spinning trying to keep up with all of the new, and sometimes conflicting, information about the content and value of certain foods. I understand that the government has just lowered the numbers for what is now considered a safe blood pressure level, and some medical researchers want to lower the borderline figure for blood sugar levels too.

Since research is constantly going on, today's facts may be tomorrow's myths. There seems to be no final word there. And we can't trust our moral instincts to determine truth, because we have been corrupted by sin. Our intellect is also a poor guide to truth, because we are finite creatures whose knowledge is extremely limited.

One way of determining truth we haven't talked about yet is just to go along with the majority. Take an opinion poll, or vote on it, and the answer with the most percentage points or votes wins. We can thank the game show *Who Wants to Be a Millionaire?* for demonstrating in prime time the fallacy of trusting the majority. I remember watching one night when a contestant used his lifeline and asked the audience for help. The audience was strongly in favor of one answer, and he went with it. But their answer was wrong, and the man lost out.

The old saying used to be that the majority can't be wrong. Sorry, but the majority is often wrong. Jesus Christ was crucified by the majority.

There is another definition of truth that rises far above the confusion and babble of our day. It is timeless and unchanging, a fixed standard by which everyone and everything can, and ultimately will, be measured.

Truth Conforms to the Nature of God

The only reason we can know any truths at all is that God is God. Truth is not just that which conforms to reality, because there is no reality apart from God. Truth is that which conforms to His nature. We as Christians can make an unapologetic, uncompromising, definitive statement about truth because of the perfectly true nature of God. The Bible calls God the Father "Him who is true" (1 John 5:20), and Jesus made the astounding statement, "I am the way, and the *truth,* and the life" (John 14:6, italics added).

Here's one example of the way God's nature is the standard for what is true. The Bible says, "God is not a man, that He should lie" (Numbers 23:19). Lying is wrong not just because it messes people up and causes harm, but because it violates God's very nature. The same can be said for murder and theft and adultery and coveting. These things are out of line with God's character. Truth and purity are part of His eternal attributes.

So while the world says truth is whatever we want to make it, God says truth must conform to a fixed standard. If I gave you a sheet of paper and a pencil and asked you to draw a straight line freehand, no matter how meticulous you were your line would not be truly straight. But if I gave you a ruler with a sharp edge to draw your line against, the outcome would be totally different. As long as your pencil follows that fixed standard, your line will be straight. And anyone else can take that same ruler and make a straight line too. Since God is by nature true, in order for something to be true it must conform to Him and His written revelation.

THE SOURCE OF TRUTH

If truth is a fixed standard of reality, and of right and wrong, that has been determined by the God who is true and unchanging, then we had better be giving careful attention to the Book He gave to communicate His truth to us.

I am not going into any elaborate arguments to prove to you that the Bible is the source of ultimate truth. We demonstrated in the previous chapter that the Bible is unique and completely worthy of the confidence we place in it, and I am going to proceed on that basis. We noted earlier Jesus' prayer: "Sanctify them in the truth; Your word is truth" (John 17:17).

Jesus made many statements like this that have staggering

implications. We talked about another one earlier, which is that, according to John 8:32, truth is knowable. The worst thing that could happen to the human race is to be cut off from the source of truth, which is why the devil works so hard either to take the Bible away from people, or take people away from the Bible.

But because God is full of grace and truth, He has revealed His Word to us so that we may walk in the truth as His children (see 3 John 4). We will study in detail the Holy Spirit's role in the process of recording God's truth, so suffice it here to say that the Spirit is called "the Spirit of truth" (John 14:17, see also 15:26; 16:13).

The Holy Spirit directed the revelation of Scripture in such a way that what was produced is pure truth from God. It could not be any other way if God is pure truth at the core of His being. Don't tell me that God wrote the Bible, but at the same time try to tell me that there are mistakes in the Bible. That is a contradiction in terms. God the Holy Spirit safeguarded the Bible, and how He did it is amazing.

God Used Human Authors to Record His Word

Whenever we say that the Bible is God's Word, the argument we often get is, "But the Bible was written by imperfect human beings who were limited in their knowledge, and they were subject to all manner of errors and mistakes."

Now the fact that the Bible was written by human authors whose lives and work are attested by history and backed by all kinds of witnesses ought to be a source of joy for us, not a problem. I say that because when you check out the cults, invariably you will find that their so-called scriptures were allegedly given to the founder in some secret, mysterious revelation that only the founder or maybe a few others experienced. In other words, no one else can verify even the process, let alone the result. But God's Word was written in the light by people who had nothing to hide and no personal heresy to promote.

That being said, we need to answer the charge that a perfect Bible cannot be the product of imperfect authors. And we do have an answer to that charge, which is that God did with the Bible what He did with His own Son in the Virgin Birth.

The Bible declares Jesus was sinless, even though a human being was the vehicle, so to speak, of His birth. How could an imperfect human being like Mary give birth to a sinless Son? Because the Holy Spirit came upon Mary (see Luke 1:35), which meant that the child in her womb was conceived by God. This ensured that Jesus was free from the contamination of sin, since the Bible says that sin entered the human race by Adam (see Romans 5:12–21). God safeguarded the purity of His Son, so that it was possible for a human being to produce a perfect result.

God Safeguarded the Truth of His Word

God did the same thing with the Bible through the process called divine inspiration. The apostle Peter, who experienced this inspiration, said the Holy Spirit oversaw the writing of Scripture so that there was no contamination in it (see 2 Peter 1:20–21). This is why we can say that God is the Bible's true Author.

But even though the Bible's human authors were "moved" or "carried along" by the Holy Spirit, they often appealed to their own experiences and witness as reliable. Peter said, "We did not follow cleverly devised tales when we made known to you the power and coming of our Lord Jesus Christ, but we were eyewitnesses of His majesty" (2 Peter 1:16). Peter went on to relate the transfiguration of Jesus, which Peter saw and heard (vv. 17–18). John, another apostolic eyewitness, wrote about "what we have heard" and "what we have seen with our eyes" (1 John 1:1).

The writers of Scripture were safeguarded from error by the Holy Spirit, who moved them to write and bore them along in the process. These men were so convinced of the truth that they were willing to die for it—which is a strong argument for the Bible's truth, by the way.

Let me tell you, even if I was part of a conspiracy to say that Jesus was the Son of God and had risen from the dead when I knew it was a lie, when people said they were going to kill me, I'd be showing them where the body was. But the writers of Scripture stood by the Word even when it meant their deaths.

THE TRUTH WITHOUT ERROR

The final point I want to make has to do with the nature of the Bible's truth. We have said that the Bible is the complete truth, and now I want to give you an important term for this doctrine. That word is *inerrant,* which means "without error." Some people will say the Bible contains truth or contains the Word of God. But that's only half the truth, because it leaves open the possibility that the Bible also contains other things.

The inerrancy of Scripture means that the Bible is true no matter what the subject. You can probably see where this takes us, because many people like to claim that the Bible is filled with historical, geographical, and scientific errors. But that's all right, these people say, because the Bible is not meant to be a textbook. All that matters is what the Bible says about matters of faith.

It's Easy to Fall Off a Slippery Slope

But this position is a "slippery slope" that can lead to all kinds of problems. For example, if God can't even get a few scientific facts straight in the Bible when He claims to be the Creator of the universe, how do we know that what He is telling us about how to reach heaven and avoid hell is the straight deal? Denying the Bible's truth on any level opens the Word up to the charge of errors everywhere.

Now at this point some Bible critic will be quick to point out that the existing manuscripts we have of the Bible vary one from another in thousands of places. So the argument goes that we can't talk about the Bible being inerrant because we don't have the original manuscripts, called the autographs.

There are two solid answers to that objection. The first has to do with human nature, and this simply is that God knows that if we had the original autographs of Scripture, we would be tempted to make an idol out of the Book and worship it instead of its Author, which would be a sin. If you don't think humans have an incurable need to make something visible to worship, go to Israel and see all the religious shrines with ornate altars and thousands of lights and candles that various Christian groups have built over the centuries at holy sites.

What about the objection that the copies of Scripture we do have contain tens of thousands of variations in words and phrasing? This is true, but the fact is that these copies do not contradict each other on the basic tenets of the faith such as the Person and work of Christ. This in itself is astounding.

It's Important to Know We Have a Perfect Standard

But the reason we still affirm the Bible's inerrancy in the autographs even though we don't have them is that it is absolutely crucial to believe and know that we have a perfect standard to work against as we compare the various existing manuscripts. Where the texts of biblical manuscripts differ, scholars work to reach the closest consensus possible on what the original said. All this work is worthwhile because it matters what the original said.

Maybe an illustration will help here. A speaker was delivering a lecture one day when a member of the audience suddenly jumped up and challenged his facts. This happened several more times before the man in the audience finally said, "If you don't have any documentation with you to show me right now, then you won't mind if I call you a liar."

The speaker replied, "OK, I see what you're saying. I don't have all of my papers with me today, but let me ask you a question. Are your father and mother legally married?"

"Of course they are!" the man replied indignantly.

"Do you have their marriage certificate with you today?"

"No, I don't."

The speaker replied, "Then you won't mind if I call *you* a liar."

You see, it is vital that we can know our faith rests on a sure foundation. It is vital that we know God spoke the truth when He spoke. Jesus made an incredibly important correlation between the spoken and written Word of God when He was tempted by the devil in the wilderness (see Matthew 4:1–11).

In the first temptation, the devil urged Jesus to turn the stones around Him into bread, since He had been fasting for forty days and was hungry. But Jesus answered, "It is written, 'Man shall not live on bread alone, but on every word that proceeds out of the mouth of God' " (v. 4). Jesus quoted from Deuteronomy 8:3, which equates the words that God spoke with His written Word. There was no difference for Jesus.

This is why Paul could affirm, "All Scripture is inspired by God" (2 Timothy 3:16). The word *inspired* means "God-breathed," which is another term for the work of the Holy Spirit as the very breath of God. If there is error anywhere in the Bible, there could be error everywhere.

It's Important to Let the Bible Speak for Itself

Now this does not mean that the Bible does not record the errors or lies of others. When a character in the Bible said or did something that was erroneous or an outright lie, the Bible faithfully records these things. But it presents them as just what they are, errors or lies. The Bible never presents a lie as the truth. So don't let someone tell you that the Bible records lies and so cannot be the whole truth.

The assertion that the Bible is inerrant also does not rule out the fact that the Word uses normal figures of speech that we use, such as talking about the rising and setting of the sun, or the hand or face of God. We know the sun doesn't rise or set, and we know that God is pure spirit. The Bible's writers wrote what God told them to write, without trying to say that the sun literally rises or that God really does have hands.

If you want a good exercise, read all of Psalm 119 in one sitting. It contains 176 verses, making it by far the longest chapter in the Bible, and it has only one subject: the majesty and wonder of God's Word. After you have finished reading Psalm 119, close your Bible and spend some time thanking God for the gift of His Word and ask Him to let it saturate your mind and heart. There is no limit to what the Word can do when we allow it to take root in our hearts, because it is always right. It will never adjust to you, but it will do wonders for you when you adjust to it.

3

THE BIBLE IS AUTHORITATIVE

It's hard for people in our culture to understand what it's like to live under the kind of absolute authority that a king or queen can wield. But that was not a problem for the subjects of King Frederick II of Prussia, known as Frederick the Great.

One man who tasted Frederick's authority was an inmate in the prison at Berlin. As the king toured the prison one day, all of the inmates loudly protested their innocence—except for one man, who said nothing.

Frederick called to the man, asking him what crime he had committed. When the man replied that it was armed robbery, the king asked, "And are you guilty?"

"Yes indeed, Your Majesty," the prisoner answered. "I entirely deserve my punishment."

Frederick was so impressed with the inmate's honest confession that he ordered him released immediately, and the man walked out of prison free.

We may read this story and think how bad it was that a convicted criminal was released. But don't miss the point. Frederick the Great had supreme authority over his subjects, and no one could undo what he decreed even if his word nullified the way things usually operated.

The supreme authority that a king holds over his subjects by virtue of his office, the Bible holds by virtue of its Author, who is the King of creation and thus Ruler over all the earth. The Bible's authority is inherent in its every word and even every portion of a word, as we will see. The Bible is supremely authoritative because it is God's revelation in history. Just as there was no higher authority that King Frederick's subjects could appeal to, there is no higher authority you and I can appeal to than the Word of God. And although the Bible may not be taken as seriously in society as it once was, a witness who takes the stand in court must still lay a hand on the Bible and take a solemn oath to tell the truth.

Now I hope you know that the Bible's authority is at the heart of many of the moral issues that threaten to tear our culture apart. For example, is the Bible authoritative for all time and every culture when it condemns homosexuality as sin? The organized church, what we would call Christendom, doesn't answer that question with a unified voice because some segments of the Christian world don't truly believe that the Bible is the supreme authority in people's lives.

Many of these church leaders may affirm their belief in the Bible. And they may appeal to the Bible's teaching on love as evidence that their approval of same-sex relationships also has God's approval. They may not say it this way, but these people really believe that in the final analysis, human interpretations stand in judgment on the Bible, rather than the Bible standing in judgment on human interpretations.

The debate over homosexuality illustrates the danger of trying to decide which parts of Scripture are authoritative as they stand, and which parts need to be amended in light of changing social standards. We need to understand that as Christians we must receive the Bible as completely reliable and trustworthy on every matter it records, or else it will eventually become nothing more than a collection of inspiring words that are nice to read but don't have the authority to direct our lives.

By the way, this matter of short-circuiting the Bible's authority isn't just a problem in the so-called liberal church. Those who consider themselves to be evangelical, Bible-believing Christians can fall into the trap of treating God's Word as little more than a book of nice stories or moral platitudes to inspire us and lift us up when we're down, rather than as God's authoritative message to us.

How can we do this? By listening politely when the Word is read or taught, then filing out of church and going about business as usual as if nothing happened. By reading the Word ourselves and yet failing to let it search and change us. By displaying the Bible on our coffee table to give everyone the impression it's the Book we live by when we know different.

Now make no mistake. The Bible can inspire and lift you up. But I can give you other books of inspirational sayings that will do the same thing. God does not simply want to inspire us by His Word. He wants us to put ourselves under its authority as the very voice of God.

THE BIBLE IS GOD'S VOICE
SPEAKING TO US TODAY

When I say the Bible is God's voice, I mean that the words of Scripture come from His mouth. This is the doctrine of inspiration, which we'll consider later. Christians talk about hearing God's voice in His Word, or hearing God speak to them through His Word. This is the Holy Spirit's ministry of illumination, another upcoming chapter in this book.

God's Voice Is Timeless in Its Authority

I want to use the term "God's voice" here to help you grasp what we might call the immediacy of the Bible's authority. That is, the

Bible's authority is timeless. For example, when we read in Exodus 20:3, "You shall have no other gods before Me," this command has the very same force behind it today that it had when God first thundered these words to Moses more than three thousand years ago. This is important because one problem I see as a pastor is that people disregard God's Word because to them, it's just ink on a page.

Our problem is that we weren't there when God first spoke His Word—because if we had been there, we wouldn't be so casual about it. To get an idea of the terror that gripped Moses and all of Israel when God gave His commandments, read Hebrews 12:18–21. Even Moses said, "I'm so scared my knees are knocking together" (v. 21, Evans translation).

Remember the day you came home from school and your mother was gone for some reason, so she left you a note about a chore she wanted done before she got back? You knew she meant what she said, but somehow that note just didn't seem to have the same authority behind it as when your mother said, "Boy, you better get that room cleaned up now!" So you disregarded the note, but when your mama got home you discovered to your pain that her written word had all of her authority behind it.

Receiving the Bible as God's voice speaking directly to us is important because of another common problem among God's people. These are the folk who know what God said, and can even repeat it back to you, but they aren't doing anything about it. Every parent is familiar with this scenario. Your child disregards your direct instructions, and when you confront that child later and say, "What did I tell you to do?" he or she can repeat your words verbatim. But for some reason your command didn't carry any weight with that child, so the result was disobedience. And a good parent won't let that go without appropriate discipline (see Hebrews 12:5–6).

Have you ever said, "I wish God would just speak to me like He did to Abraham or Moses"? Well, there are two answers to that wish.

First, you don't really mean it, because if God did speak to you the way He spoke to Moses, your heart probably would not survive the experience. When even angels spoke in the Bible, people trembled and fell down.

Second, and more important, God *has* spoken to you and me in His Word. It is His voice. So when we open our Bibles, maybe we should start saying, "I am going to listen to God's voice speak to me today."

Jesus Used the Bible to Affirm His Deity

Jesus was being challenged by His opponents one day when He tried to tell them that He was God. They objected, accused Him of blasphemy, and got ready to stone Him (see John 10:31–33). Jesus turned to the Scripture to make His case, and the way He used the Word has a lot to teach us about the Bible's authority.

"Jesus answered them, 'Has it not been written in your Law, "I said, you are gods"?' If he called them gods, to whom the word of God came (*and the Scripture cannot be broken*), do you say of Him, whom the Father sanctified and sent into the world, 'You are blaspheming,' because I said, 'I am the Son of God'?" (vv. 34–36, italics added).

Jesus was using a powerful argument here. He said that if the Bible—in this case the psalmist Asaph (Psalm 82:6)—used the term *gods* for men who were merely God's representatives, then those who were accusing Jesus should not object if He called Himself God. Why? Because they had just seen Him heal a blind man (John 9) and do other miracles, for one thing.

What I want you to see here is the binding authority of Scripture. Not even one word can be changed. Let me give you a term you may not have encountered before. Scripture is irrefragable, which means it cannot be voided or invalidated. How important is this trait of Holy Writ? It was important enough to Jesus that He built a critical argument around it.

The Lord's opponents might have wished they could nullify or get around the word *gods* in Psalm 82:6, because it is the Hebrew word *Elohim*, which is one of the names of God. But Jesus had them, because God's Word called His representatives "gods," and nothing could change the Scripture. Paul used a similar tactic in Galatians 3 to prove that Jesus is Abraham's promised seed. The validity of Paul's entire point hung on the difference between the singular "seed" and the plural "seeds" (v. 16). Not only each letter of the Bible, but even the smallest part of each letter (see Matthew 5:18), is vital and carries God's authority.

Jesus Said the Bible Carries His Authority

Jesus Christ also said that the Bible carries the imprint of His divine authority. He announced to His disciples, "Heaven and earth will pass away, but My words will not pass away" (Matthew 24:35). That statement on the lips of anyone other than Jesus would be heresy, but He alone can claim, "All authority has been given to Me in heaven and on earth" (Matthew 28:18). Therefore, Jesus' words, which are recorded in Scripture, will outlast history, because the Word is eternal. I love the way the psalmist put it: "Forever, O Lord, Your word is settled in heaven" (Psalm 119:89).

Now I don't know about you, but this raises a question in my mind. Since Jesus possesses all authority, and His Word has all of His authority behind it, why are we as Christians not seeing God's Word at work any more than we are? I am convinced the reason is that we are not living as though God's Word were our authority. We are not seeing more power in our lives and in the church at large because we aren't taking the Bible seriously. To paraphrase the Nike commercials, we fail to "just do it."

This reminds me of the wedding in Cana of Galilee at which Jesus performed His first miracle (John 2:1–11). It's interesting that even though Jesus commanded all of creation, He didn't mind going to an ordinary, everyday wedding. Our Lord never tried to hang out with the elite and show off His power.

You'll remember that at this wedding in Cana, they ran out of wine and Mary told Jesus about the problem (v. 3). Even though Jesus seemed to deny Mary's request, she told the servants at the wedding, "Whatever He says to you, do it" (v. 5). In other words, "This man has the authority to ask anything He wants of you."

This is worth noticing because Jesus had not told them what to do yet. Mary didn't know that Jesus was going to give the servants an order that didn't seem to make sense, which was to fill the stone jars with water. All she knew was if Jesus acted, something powerful would happen.

Do you see where I'm going? We often say to God, in our actions if not always in our words, "Show me what You want me to do first, and then I'll decide whether I want to do it." Of course, there is nothing wrong with asking God to show you His will. But He never reveals His will so we can discuss and debate it. God is into obedience, not just presenting options. Jesus' power to turn water into wine at Cana was activated when the servants obeyed Him. And the beautiful part of the story is that the wine Jesus made was better than anything they had ever tasted before.

Have you ever run into something God is asking you to do that you don't want to do? And worst of all, it doesn't even seem to make sense? But if God is calling you to obey, don't try to figure it out. Don't go asking everybody else what you should do. Don't take a vote and see how many other folk would agree with you. Just do what God says.

Rejecting the Bible Means Rejecting Jesus

If Jesus Christ tied His authority so closely to the Bible's authority, then the logical conclusion is that to reject the authority of Scripture is to reject Christ.

We saw earlier in John 10:34–36 that Jesus appealed to the authority and inviolability of the Bible to argue that He was correct in saying, "I and the Father are one" (v. 30). His detractors understood very clearly that Jesus was claiming to be God, and they wanted to stone Him for blasphemy (vv. 31–33) because Jesus was claiming an authority they said no one but God should be able to claim. And they were exactly right. Jesus could only claim this authority because He was God in the flesh.

Jesus answered their charge by showing them that they could not reject Him without rejecting the Word of God they professed to believe. He pointed to the works He had done (vv. 37–38) as proof of His deity, knowing the Jews believed that Messiah would do great miracles when He came (see John 3:2).

You can't say you love and believe God's Word without loving and believing the Savior whom God has sent. It is said of Jesus in the Gospels that He spoke "as one having authority, and not as [the] scribes" (Matthew 7:29). The scribes had opinions and their Jewish traditions, but Jesus spoke with the voice of God, and we have His words in the Bible.

WE MUST RESPOND TO GOD'S VOICE TO US IN THE BIBLE

The fact that the Bible is completely authoritative and cannot be broken is a wonderful doctrine of the Christian faith. But the truth and power of God's Word can be nullified in your experience if you refuse to let the Word speak to you as it is or you start mixing it up with your human viewpoints.

Now please notice that I did not say the Bible can lose its power or authority. That will never happen because God said His Word is "forever settled in heaven." But the Bible's power is blunted in our lives when we do not respond to God in humility and obedience.

Don't Mix the Bible's Words with Your Words

This is probably the number one travesty that people who claim to believe and follow God's Word commit against it. A lot of people who try to mix their own thoughts with the Bible's teaching have many degrees after their name. Education is fine, and the church has benefited from well-trained commentators and scholars who seek to understand what the Word means.

This is not what I'm talking about. There's a big difference between an honest attempt to understand the Bible as it reads and diluting its teachings with human thinking. The best example of this is in Scripture itself, when the Pharisees and scribes came to Jesus to accuse His disciples of breaking "the tradition of the elders" (Matthew 15:1–2).

But Jesus came back at them with a much more serious charge, that of nullifying the Word of God (vv. 4–6), using the example of God's commandment to honor one's father and mother. Jesus showed how the scribes and Pharisees allowed people, mainly themselves, to get around this clear command with a hollow promise to give those resources to God while actually not having to give them away at all.

Jesus gave the bottom line of this kind of thinking when He said at the end of verse 6, "And by this you invalidated the word of God for the sake of your tradition." The point is that God never meant for the commandment to honor your father and mother to be skirted on a technicality.

The Jews added so many traditions and regulations to the Law that they ended up creating a barrier around the Word so people couldn't get to it. Now let's give them enough credit to say that they were trying to help God out. And there were questions that had to be worked out in everyday life. But these rules became more important than what God said.

The Bible says, "Let God be found true, though every man be found a liar" (Romans 3:4). The issue Jesus dealt with was the authority of God's Word. If God says we are to honor our parents, then trying to find a "loophole" in that command is a sin against the truth.

This thing of truth and authority is at the core of why the Holy Spirit is not doing more in our lives. The Spirit is the Spirit of truth who is obligated only to God's Word. So when we start diluting the Word with our human viewpoints, the Spirit steps back, because He is not going to bless our speculations.

Just before the closing benediction in Revelation, we find a dual warning to anyone who either "adds to" or "takes away from" the words of this book (Revelation 22:18–19). God pronounces a curse when people start messing with His message. God doesn't need anyone to help Him say what He wants to say.

I think of this because I'm one of those people who anticipates what I think others are going to say in a conversation and then helps them out by finishing their sentence for them. Sometimes the other person will say, "No, that's not what I meant at all." I took the wrong train trying to anticipate their train of thought and wound up in the wrong station.

Well, God is not looking for our help to finish His sentences. Everything He wanted said, He preserved in the pages of His Word. The reason the Spirit is not free to work His supernatural activity in our lives is that we are dealing with mixed truth, the Word diluted by human thinking. You know you have run into this when you hear someone say, "I know what the Bible says about this, but . . ." In other words, this person's case is different. He's the exception.

Don't Poison the Pot of Stew

There's an interesting story in 2 Kings 4:38–41 about the prophet Elisha and the "apprentice prophets" who were under his tutelage. There was a famine in the land, and these student prophets were hungry. Elisha told his servant to make a pot of stew for everybody, and one of the prophets gathered some wild gourds for the stew. The gourds looked fine to him, and he probably thought they would add a little spice to the stew. So he decided to help out by tossing the gourds into the stew.

But as everyone ate, some apparently began to feel sick and said the stew was poisoned. Someone cried out to Elisha, "O man of God, there is death in the pot" (v. 40). Elisha took care of the problem, and the stew was fine.

This story helps to explain why, for instance, we don't let just anyone take the pulpit and preach in our church. Our church is committed to the truth and authority of God's Word, and our people don't need to be getting sick from someone who thinks he is helping God out by adding to what God has said.

Unfortunately, this happens every Sunday in churches all across this nation. Plenty of pastors and teachers are tossing "wild gourds" into the pot—adding human wisdom to God's Word or even allowing human views and opinions to replace the Scriptures. This is why people can actually be worse off by going to church, because they come away more confused and unsure than ever about whether the Bible is even true, let alone whether it has any relevance to them.

Now you may say, "Don't worry, Tony. I don't go to a church like that. Our pastor and other teachers believe and teach the Bible faithfully."

Praise God for that. But you can still "get sick" spiritually even in a good church by tossing your own wild gourds of human opinion into the Word. I often hear people say, "My mama taught me," or "All my friends say."

Well, godly mothers certainly have a lot to teach us. And friends can help us see things in a different light. But before you listen to what other people are saying, check it against what God says. A lot of the advice people get is given by folk who aren't even living out their own advice. Don't let someone else spoil the effect of the Word in your life with the poison of human opinion.

Take Your Bible Out of the Museum

I mentioned in a previous chapter that the French atheist Voltaire boasted that by the time he was done, the only Bibles left would be museum pieces. He was spectacularly wrong, but I must say that as a pastor I have seen many Bibles in museums.

I'm not talking about the British Museum or some other great holder of ancient biblical manuscripts. I'm talking about the "museum" of people's houses, or even their cars. Many Christians have Bibles on the shelf at home. A lot of people have a Bible for every room of the house, and I've also seen a lot of Bibles in the back windows of cars. But these places are museums if the Bibles never get taken off the shelf and read.

There used to be a day when having a big Bible on the coffee table was impressive, but that's not a big deal anymore. I love the story of the woman who was being visited by her pastor. She wanted to impress him, so she said to her daughter, "Honey, go get that wonderful book that Mama loves so much and reads from every day. You know, the book Mama keeps on her nightstand." The little girl ran off and came back with the Sears catalog!

Let God Set Your Life's Agenda

Biblical authority means that God has the supreme right to determine our decision making and set the agenda for our lives. God doesn't want our rationalizations, but our response. He wants us to do like we do when we're driving and come up over a hill only to see a police car sitting on the side of the road.

That police car is a symbol of the officer's authority—and we know the officer also has the clout to back up that authority. So if we are doing wrong by speeding, we don't just say, "Big deal. So what if I'm doing eighty in a fifty-five zone? I don't need to do anything."

No, when we see the police car and we know we are not living right at that moment, our heart starts to palpitate and we hit the brake. Why? Because we have run into a legitimate authority that we respect, and we respond. In other words, the presence of this authority creates a response, not just an analysis.

Paul told Timothy to preach the Word whether it was convenient or not because people would want to have "their ears tickled" instead of hearing the truth (2 Timothy 4:2–3). There's nothing wrong with feeling good, as long as it's the truth that is making you feel good. But when a lie is making you feel good, it's illegitimate.

Too many people treat the Bible the way Great Britain treats the queen. The British people give great honor to the queen, and she is involved in many impressive and elaborate displays of her power and authority. But when it comes to governing the country, the queen is for show only, because England is a constitutional monarchy. The queen is the representative head of the land, but she is just a figurehead. She doesn't make or veto laws, and she doesn't formulate policy. The queen has no real authority. She doesn't set the agenda for her country.

People can have Bibles in every room of the house, in their cars, and even at their offices, and yet still want to have their ears tickled by the latest religious fad or clever deceiver. But God wants to occupy the place of supreme authority in your life, and He wants to set your life's agenda as you submit yourself to His Word.

4

THE
BIBLE
IS
POWERFUL

In March 2003, President George Bush ended months of specu-
lation about whether American forces would attack Saddam Hussein's regime in Iraq, when a method called "Shock and Awe" was
launched. The president is reported to have authorized the massive attack by uttering two words: "Let's go." On March 19, the skies
over Baghdad began lighting up as the U.S.–led aerial attack began.

How could two simple words like "Let's go" send the greatest military force on earth and its coalition partners into action? What was
it about this brief command that generated enough power to bring
down a dictator and send him into a hole in the ground to hide?

We know why the words "Let's go" had so much power behind
them. It's because they came from the lips of the president of the
United States and commander in chief of our armed forces. President Bush holds the most powerful position in the world, and therefore his words have the power of his office behind them. When the

president gave the order, folk weren't sitting around yawning, ignoring what he said, or trying to figure out if he really meant what he said. The president is a powerful person with a determined purpose, and the people under his command fall in line with his will.

I drew out this analogy a little more because I want to set the scene for our study in this chapter. The Word of God can transform any situation or person, because built into it is the ability to pull off whatever God desires it to accomplish. Power is the ability to affect change or produce the desired effect. This is a good working definition of what I mean by the power of God's Word.

A key Scripture passage that teaches this truth is one of the verses from that great section of Isaiah 55 we quoted in the opening chapter. Verse 11 says, "So will My word be which goes forth from My mouth; it will not return to Me empty, without accomplishing what I desire, and without succeeding in the matter for which I sent it."

The unstoppable power of God's Word is another attribute that sets it apart from anyone else's word. When God had finished giving Job a lesson in His awesome power, Job confessed: "I know that You can do all things, and that no purpose of Yours can be thwarted" (Job 42:2). The prophet agreed, saying, "For the Lord of hosts has planned, and who can frustrate it?" (Isaiah 14:27).

We humans spew out a lot of words, and people make all manner of boasts, promises, and threats. But a lot of what we say never comes to pass, for which we can be thankful. Our plans are frustrated all the time because we are not all-powerful. And a lot of people talk just to show everyone that they are in charge, but their attempts to throw their weight around have no real purpose behind them. These are the kind of people who often answer the question, "Why are you doing this?" with, "Just because I can."

God's Word has neither of these shortcomings. It cannot be frustrated or stopped, and God never goes around showing off His power just because He can. His Word is always purposeful when it goes out from His mouth, and that purpose is always achieved. God's power is never random or out of control. He always has a plan that He intends to fulfill.

I want to give you two great biblical examples of the power that God's Word has to accomplish His purposes. We could call these the Bible's external and internal power, because they refer to the creation around us and our soul and spirit at the innermost recesses of our beings. The word that God spoke, as revealed and preserved in the Bible, can bring a world into being and cut to the core of our hearts.

GOD'S WORD HAS
THE POWER TO CREATE A UNIVERSE

When the writers of Scripture wanted to illustrate the awesome power of God, they often pointed to His creation of the world. The psalmist declared, "By the word of the Lord the heavens were made, and by the breath of His mouth all their host" (Psalm 33:6). Then he added in verse 9, "For He spoke, and it was done; He commanded, and it stood fast," referring to the earth and all of its mighty oceans.

God Can Make Something Out of Nothing

To simply speak a world into existence is power beyond anything we can imagine. Theologians have a phrase for the creative act of God whereby He made the universe out of nothing. It is called creation *ex nihilo,* or "out of nothing." In other words, God did not need any raw materials to work with when He created the world. He created the raw materials and everything else with His word.

I've seen the Taj Mahal in India and Buckingham Palace in London. They are incredible feats of architecture, but the builders had to have the raw materials with which to build. Even Rumplestiltskin in the children's fairy tale had to have straw to spin into gold.

But Genesis 1 records again and again that "God said . . . and it was so." This is creation *ex nihilo,* making not just something out of nothing, but *everything* out of nothing. We hear about people making something out of nothing in terms of rescuing a project that is going nowhere, or putting together a business deal or maybe even a treaty when all hopes for an agreement seemed to be over.

Of course, no human being can literally make something out of nothing—unless we count the evolutionists! Nor can we just speak and make whatever we want happen. You may be able to make lemonade out of a lemon, but at least you have to start with a lemon. My wife can put together a bunch of leftovers, make a little gravy to cover them, and serve the best meal you never knew you already had. But she has to have some leftovers to work her special touch on.

But God spoke just two words in the Hebrew text of Genesis 1:3, which could be translated "Light be," and light appeared. He spoke again and the dry land appeared. Time after time, God said the word and whatever He commanded came into being. There were no gaps or lapses. God simply worked out His will through His word.

You've never seen power like this before. As commander in chief, the president of the United States can speak two words and set a great military machine in motion. But as commander in chief of the universe, God's two words created the sun.

God Can Create Life Out of Death

I like the way Paul put it. He said that God "calls into being that which does not exist" (Romans 4:17). The apostle made this great statement of God's power in the middle of discussing Abraham's faith in God's promise to give him a child even though he and Sarah were way too old to become parents. In fact, the Bible says that in terms of their ability to bear children, both Sarah and Abraham were as good as dead (v. 19).

That was no problem for God. His word to Abraham was, "I will surely return to you at this time next year; and behold, Sarah your wife will have a son" (Genesis 18:10). This was God's promise to Abraham, and it came to pass.

The power of God's Word was on display in an even greater way in the birth of Jesus Christ, who was the fulfillment of the promised Son of which Isaac was a type. Luke 1:26–38 is an incredible passage of Scripture that tells of the angel Gabriel announcing to Mary that she was going to have a baby. Mary was stunned at this word, and wondered how this could be since she was a virgin. This was an impossible situation as far as Mary was concerned.

You know the rest of the story. Gabriel informed Mary that she would be with child by the Holy Spirit, so the One she bore would be a miraculous child. And not only that, but Gabriel let Mary know that she was not the only one God was working with. He informed Mary that her older relative Elizabeth was already six months into her pregnancy, even though she and her husband Zacharias had never been able to conceive and she was now too old to have children.

I want you to see the last two verses of Gabriel's conversation with Mary. After announcing that Elizabeth was expecting a child, the angel said to Mary, "For nothing will be impossible with God" (Luke 1:37). Mary had hardly had time to absorb the startling news that she was going to conceive and bear the Savior of the world, and now she was being told that Elizabeth was going to have a baby too.

At least Elizabeth had a husband, and her baby had come about by means of human conception, just as Isaac was fathered by Abraham. However, Elizabeth's conception of John the Baptist was still a miracle because she was old and her womb was as dead as Sarah's. But when it came to the virgin Mary and the birth of Jesus, we have the miracle of all miracles.

The angel had the message that made sense out of all this for Mary: "For nothing will be impossible with God." Now let me show you something interesting about this verse. The word *nothing* here actually translates three words in the Greek text that literally mean "not any word." The idea is that no word God speaks is too hard for Him to fulfill. So the fact that Mary was a virgin was no obstacle to God.

We said earlier that when God exercises His power, it is always purposeful. The angel explained God's purpose in giving Mary a son: "He will be great and will be called the Son of the Most High; and the Lord God will give Him the throne of His father David; and He will reign over the house of Jacob forever, and His kingdom will have no end" (Luke 1:32–33).

The angel's point was that God was working out a plan. In order to accomplish this plan He needed a virgin, because no human father could be involved. Mary thought she was in an impossible situation, but God didn't want her to focus on the impossibility because that word is not in His vocabulary. Mary got the point and said, "May it be done to me according to your word" (v. 38). End of conversation.

God Can Make Something Where You See Nothing

Now the fact that God can speak and make it so ought to be good news when you look at your circumstances and don't see any way that anything can happen. You read in your Bible that God says He can do anything, but nothing is changing at your place of work or at home. That's when you need to remember that God doesn't need anything to do His work, because His Word is powerful. No word that He speaks is impossible for Him to do. And all of God's authority stands behind the Bible.

This means it doesn't matter who tries to stop God from carrying out the Word He has spoken. The Enemy can throw up a lot of defenses, and may even appear to be winning sometimes because God allows human choices and failings to be part of His plan. But God guarantees that even these things will be incorporated into His divine program. No matter how long it takes or what has to happen to get there, God will accomplish His objective. His Word is sure and effective.

Now don't misunderstand. I'm not saying there is some kind of special power in the pieces of paper stitched together between leather to make a Bible. One charge that liberal theologians and churchmen make against evangelicals is that we worship the Bible instead of worshiping God.

No, we worship the God who has revealed Himself to us in His Word. The Bible is like the electrical outlet in your home that puts you in touch with the power source when you plug into it. Without the power, the plug would be dead—which, by the way, is the problem with every other so-called holy book in the world. They lack power because they are just human words on a page. The plug is dead, so to speak.

God's Word Sustains What He Has Created

God not only brought the universe into existence by the power of His Word, but that same Word also sustains His creation. The writer of Hebrews said of Jesus, "He is the radiance of [God's] glory and the exact representation of His nature, and upholds all things by the word of His power" (1:3). God is able to sustain what He brings into being (see 2 Peter 3:5–7).

This is part of the good news of our salvation. As the gospel song puts it, God didn't bring you this far just to leave you. The reason you can't lose your salvation is that what God creates, He keeps. If you are a Christian, you are a new creation in Christ (see 2 Corinthians 5:17), and no one can snatch you out of God's hand (see John 10:28–30).

You've probably heard it said that plants grow better when you talk to them. Well, apparently it has been scientifically demonstrated that this is true, even though most of us thought only crazy folk talked to their plants.

How can talking to plants help them? What happens is that when you speak, you take in oxygen and release carbon dioxide. According to a scientific study, when you speak close to a plant it absorbs the carbon dioxide from the breath going out of your mouth.

When I read that, I said to myself, "Oh, I feel an illustration coming on." When your breath goes out, the carbon dioxide you release enters the plant and has the power to produce something good that the plant needs to grow. Now if human words have the power to help sustain a plant, what do you think can happen when the Word goes out from God's mouth? His Word has the power to enter all of creation and sustain it, including you and me. If God can plant the seed of His eternal, pre-existent Son in a virgin's womb, then nothing else is impossible for Him to do.

GOD'S WORD HAS THE POWER TO SEARCH US

Now we're getting down to the nitty-gritty. From the vastness of creation we are going to focus down to the inner workings of the human soul and spirit. God's Word has the power to pierce into the deepest recesses of our being with laserlike power and precision.

We know this from a great passage of Scripture that I hope is familiar to you: "For the word of God is living and active and sharper than any two-edged sword, and piercing as far as the division of soul and spirit, of both joints and marrow, and able to judge the thoughts and intentions of the heart. And there is no creature hidden from His sight, but all things are open and laid bare to the eyes of Him with whom we have to do" (Hebrews 4:12–13).

God's Spirit Is Active in His Word

The Bible is not dead words on a page, but is alive and powerful, which is the idea behind the word *active*. The Bible is a living document because it is the Word of the living God, animated by the living Holy Spirit. Genesis 1:2 says that God's Spirit was "moving," or hovering, over the waters of the earth at creation, breathing life into the creation.

The Holy Spirit does the same thing with the Word that He did with creation. The Spirit hovers over the Word and breathes life into it, with the result that we are not to read the Bible the way we read a novel, a history book, or any other book. We read other books to get information or to be entertained, but we should read the Bible to get life from it and allow it to penetrate our hearts.

As a pastor I am often asked by people how they can know when the Bible is really beginning to come alive to them. My answer is simple. You know the Bible is alive to you when it begins to cut on you, because that's what Hebrews 4:12 says the Word is designed to do.

God's Word Cuts to the Heart

The writer of Hebrews likened the Bible to a two-edged sword that cuts on both sides as it is thrust into the target. Roman soldiers carried these swords, which were kept very sharp. When a Roman soldier used his two-edged sword on an enemy, it penetrated deeply for maximum effect.

Now if this imagery seems a little graphic to you, you're getting the idea. God's Word is so sharp and powerful that it can plunge into our spirits like a sharp sword that cuts not even just to the bone, but into the marrow inside the bone. No other book can reach down into a person that deeply and bring about the effects that the Bible can.

In other words, God wants His Word to do spiritual surgery on us. He wants to lay bare our souls so He can show us what's on the inside of us. Have you ever said or done something that seemed out of character for you, and you wondered later where in the world that came from? Maybe it was there all the time.

All of us are capable of reacting in ways that are unusual for us, but at the same time we don't really know our own hearts very well. The Bible says, "The heart is more deceitful than all else and is desperately sick; who can understand it?" (Jeremiah 17:9). The answer is that no one can understand the human heart perfectly—no one, that is, except God. He knows our deepest thoughts because our souls and spirits are completely exposed before Him.

This explains why people testify that when they read the Bible, they feel as if it is looking into the deepest recesses of their minds and hearts. They feel this because the Word is alive and powerful, constantly probing us. It's a good thing to be probed and exposed by the incision that God makes in our lives by His Word, because that's when we really deal with deep-rooted sin and begin to grow.

How would you feel if you went into your bathroom one evening during a party you were hosting and found some of your guests going through your medicine chest and every drawer in your bathroom, checking out your stuff and showing each other what they found? What if you went into your office or den and found other guests discussing your checkbook, reading your journal, and rifling through every folder in your personal file cabinet?

You would feel violated, and rightly so, because your guests have no right or authority to dig into your personal life at that kind of intimate level. Their probing is illegitimate, but God has the authority to search us by His Word because He made and redeemed us.

Let God's Word Do Its Work in You

Make no mistake about it. One of the most risky things you can do is give the Holy Spirit permission to open you up and do spiritual surgery on you. But it's also one of the most important things you can do, for the same reason that it's important to give your doctor permission to operate on you when you have something that needs to be fixed or removed. It isn't until you submit to the surgeon's knife that real healing can take place.

It's amazing that medical science has such sophisticated equipment that doctors can look inside a human heart while it is beating to see what is going on. Doctors can now see things that may be hidden from sight, but that can kill you.

A skilled heart specialist doesn't just look into your heart like an impartial observer who simply records what he sees without making any judgments or decisions. The doctor critiques, or evaluates, the situation based on what his examination reveals.

Hebrews 4:12 says that God's Word does the same thing. It critiques "the thoughts and intentions of the heart." That's what the word *judge* means. It is the word for a critic. A drama critic watches a play and then makes judgments about what is good, what needs to be improved, and what needs to be discarded.

We may assume that most of our thoughts and intentions, or plans, are fine. But we are ultimately not capable of making that judgment. We need the Holy Spirit to take the sword of the Word and slice us open right down to the core of our being. We need to separate what is good from what is worthless, the way a person in Bible times would winnow wheat to separate it from the chaff, so the good wheat would be saved and the bad chaff would blow away in the wind.

The Word of God is living and powerful, and what God wants to do is show us the power of His Word. Through the Word you will come to see yourself as God sees you, which is as you really are. You will also come to see God in ways that you could not see Him otherwise. And when God begins to stitch you up after performing spiritual surgery, you will come back from the operation stronger than ever.

Experience the Power of God's Word

Someone may say, "I'm not sure if I know what you're talking about. I read the Bible, but I've never experienced anything like what you've been describing."

I've been a pastor long enough to know that many Christians feel this way, even if they don't say so. One reason the Bible may not seem to have any power in our lives is that we are not using it in accordance with God's purposes for His Word.

What I mean is that if we are reading the Word just so we can say we've had our devotions, because we feel like we're supposed to, or because the preacher said we should, then we are going to miss the purpose God has for us. God's purpose is that His Word go into our deepest parts and begin to remake us from the inside out, conforming us to the image of Christ (see Romans 8:29).

The power of God's Word is discovered as we cooperate with the purposes for which God gave us His Word. The Word will always accomplish God's will, which is good and perfect (see Romans 12:2). The only question still on the floor is whether we are going to get in on the action.

5

THE
BIBLE
IS
SUFFICIENT

Go into almost any bookstore today and you will probably find books that include the word *Bible* in their title. You'll also find books that, while they might not contain the actual word, have been called "the bible" on their particular subject, such as the vegetarian's bible or the fashion bible. I understand there is even a hunter's bible.

Why would an author or a publisher want to call a book the such-and-such "bible"? Why would a reviewer refer to a book, or perhaps a magazine or some other publication, as the "bible" in that field? They do it because the Bible is associated with the final word on a subject. The idea is that this publication contains everything that anyone will ever need to know about the topic at hand. So when you see the vegetarian bible, the author is trying to tell you that everything you need to know about being a victorious vegetarian is contained within the pages of his book.

We might think this is a backhanded tribute to the Bible, but it is a tribute nonetheless. Every time someone in the publishing world uses the word *bible* to describe his product, he is giving an unintentional witness to the doctrine known as the sufficiency of Scripture. The Bible's sufficiency means that God's Word is comprehensive in its ability to speak to every area and every need in life. There is no issue we will ever face that is not addressed either by direct command or by general principle in the Word. I can guarantee you that the vegetarian bible or the fashion bible has left out something pertaining to its field. But in the Bible, God has given us "everything pertaining to life and godliness" (2 Peter 1:3).

I've been preaching the Bible since I was eighteen years old, and yet I feel like I have only begun to tap into the endless vein of truth in God's Word. Every time I go to the Word there is something new I didn't see before, something deep I didn't understand. In other words, the Bible is inexhaustible in scope and thus sufficient for life.

Someone has said that while the Bible is so deep that theologians can spend a lifetime plumbing its depths, it is so simple a child can read and understand it. The sufficiency of Scripture is such that every age can learn from its teachings. Paul put this doctrine into a compact statement when he wrote: "All Scripture is inspired by God and profitable for teaching [or doctrine], for reproof, for correction, for training [or instruction] in righteousness; so that the man of God may be adequate, equipped for every good work" (2 Timothy 3:16–17).

One magnificent passage of Scripture lays out the sufficiency of the Word in very beautiful and clear terms. In Psalm 19:7–14, the psalmist David made six statements about the ability of God's revelation to address every area of human existence, and in particular every area that we as believers need to know if we are going to please God. These verses also speak to the all-consuming desire we should have for the Word, and remind us that God's Word can keep us from sin.

Verses 1–6 of Psalm 19 form a backdrop to this poetic tribute to the Word, and we need to review them briefly. They deal with general revelation, the truth about God that He has written, so to speak, into every atom of creation and made available to every person. The psalm begins with a declaration of this truth: "The heavens are telling of the glory of God; and their expanse is declaring the work of His hands" (v. 1).

In other words, even someone who can't read or doesn't have a Bible can still know beyond a doubt that there is a God. The reality of God ought to be clear simply by observing the world around us. The Bible never spends time defending God's existence, but says instead, "The fool has said in his heart, 'There is no God'" (Psalm 14:1). People have to be taught not to believe in God, because it is natural for human beings to look around them and above them and conclude that someone bigger and more powerful than they made all of this. It's also natural for people to worship or at least try to placate the God they know is there.

Just reading Psalm 19:1–6 makes it clear that God's revelation of Himself in creation is powerful and profound. But general revelation is also limited. It is enough to condemn the sinner, as Paul said in Romans 1:18–23. In fact, those who reject or pervert this witness in nature are "without excuse" (v. 20) because they did not follow it to its logical conclusion, which is to seek the God of whom it speaks.

But general revelation is limited because it is not sufficient in and of itself to save the sinner. Psalm 19:3 says of the heavens as God's witness, "There is no speech, nor are there words; their voice is not heard." We can look at the stars or the oceans and know that the creator God must be great and powerful. But we must go to His Word to learn that He has spoken to us and revealed that He is altogether righteous and judges sin, and is the Father of our Lord Jesus Christ.

We can be eternally grateful that Psalm 19 does not end with verse 6—or that Romans 1 does not contain only condemnation, for that matter. Let's consider this psalm's six declarations about the glorious sufficiency of God's Word.

THE BIBLE IS GOD'S PERFECT GUIDE FOR US

David began what we could call this hymn of praise to God by saying, "The law of the Lord is perfect, restoring the soul" (Psalm 19:7a). "Law" is another term for the Scripture. David must have wanted to begin at the top, because he described the Word of God as perfect. This term refers to that which is whole, complete, not lacking in any area. The Bible is complete in its revelation of divine truth.

There Are No Flaws in God's Word

Now let me clarify something here before we go any further. To say that the Bible is complete is not to claim that God has told us everything. We know that isn't so. The apostle John said that if everything Jesus did while He was on earth was recorded, even "the world itself" could not contain the books this would require (John 21:25). And John was just talking about a three-year slice of time.

The Bible says, "The secret things belong to the Lord our God" (Deuteronomy 29:29). His knowledge is inexhaustible. If God told us everything, we would be like Him. Much of what the Lord has for us will have to wait until we are with Him in heaven. But in the meantime, God's revealed Word has everything we need to know to be all that God expects us to be.

God's Word Has Power to Restore Us

The second half of this phrase in Psalm 19:7a gives us the blessing or benefit of His perfect Word: It restores the soul. This is a picture of something being brought back to its original condition. It speaks of being revived or refreshed. The Bible is sufficient to take what is broken and restore it, much like you might restore an old piece of furniture to its original beauty. God's Word can make old things new.

What is your soul? The Hebrew word *nephesh* refers to the

essence of your being, who you are at your core. Most of us spend most of our time trying to fix what we do rather than who we are. But we only do what we do because we are who we are. God's Word deals with our whole being, and it has the power to turn us inside out so we can see ourselves the way He sees us.

Now that's often a painful process, because many people who look great on the outside are broken, bruised, and battered on the inside. An insightful little poem says, "If every man's internal woe were written on his brow, how many who our envy know would have our pity now."

All of us have scars on our souls, but God's Word can heal us on the inside. And this is not just true of salvation. Christians need spiritual healing too. As someone has said, salvation cleanses us from sin, but it doesn't cure us of sin. Paul said our sin-contaminated bodies are decaying every day, but I love what he added: "Yet our inner man is being renewed day by day" (2 Corinthians 4:16). Paul's words are a great confirmation of what David was saying in Psalm 19.

Get the Benefits of God's Word

Now let me tell you something. You can't have a provision this awesome and comprehensive and not take full advantage of it. You can't have a promise and a guarantee this sweet and just leave it lying there on the table.

It was easy for me to encourage my youngest son, Jonathan, during his high school football career. First of all, I love football and I knew that Jonathan loved it too. Second, I didn't want to have to pay for college, and Jonathan was good enough to have a shot at getting a scholarship.

Well, Jonathan got a football scholarship to Baylor University, and I got my praise on because as of this writing, Baylor is about $20,000 a year! Not only did the scholarship provide a "full ride" for Jonathan with everything paid, but I could see him play in Waco, less than one hundred miles away.

I know you will agree with me that it would be a shame to have a comprehensive, all-sufficient provision like that and not take full advantage of it. Jonathan was red-shirted, or held out of competition, his first year in college, so at this point he still has one year of eligibility left even though he will graduate before his final football season. But he is planning to pursue further studies, which will also provide him with a fourth year of football.

Now all together, that's about five years of college at $20,000 a pop. You can do the math. That's why when my son comes home saying, "I'm tired," or says he's thinking about taking it easy with fewer hours than he needs to maintain his scholarship, I don't want to hear about it. Not when he has a scholarship that valuable. You can't have a gift like that and not use it.

The same is true many times over for the gift we have in God's Word. The Bible can restore you if you will avail yourself of its benefits.

THE BIBLE CAN MAKE US WISE

Psalm 19:7 goes on to make a second statement about the Word of God. "The testimony of the Lord is sure, making wise the simple."

God's testimony refers to His truth as revealed in Scripture. The statements a witness makes in court are supposed to be nothing but the truth, but only God's witness is 100 percent true. Thus it is completely solid, or trustworthy. You can build your life on it. That's what the psalmist meant when he said the Word is "sure" like a rock, as opposed to something unstable and flimsy.

We Need to Be Wise in God's Estimation

Jesus used this contrast in His famous story of the wise man who built his house on the rock and the foolish man who built on sand (see Matthew 7:24–27). The rock held firm in the storm, while the sand gave way because it was ultimately an unreliable foundation. The difference between the two men in Jesus' story was whether they heeded or ignored His Word. That's what makes a person wise in the biblical sense. Wisdom is the ability to live life skillfully under God.

I don't know any Christian who doesn't want to be wise. Even many unbelievers want to make what they consider to be wise choices. What does the Bible mean when it calls someone simple? It doesn't mean somebody who is stupid or lacks intellect. The simple person in the Bible is one who doesn't know how to make good choices. It is the person whose judgment or ability to discern things from a godly standpoint is flawed. The simple person doesn't know how to set the right boundaries, or how to position himself under God correctly. So he goes ahead somewhat blindly, doing what seems best at the moment.

All of us make unwise decisions at times. Some of the choices we have made would have been different if we knew before the decision what we learned after making it. Maybe we didn't calculate the data correctly, or investigate it thoroughly enough. Maybe we were too immature at that point in our lives, and so we were unsure of ourselves and did not exercise good judgment.

It Is Imperative to "Choose Wisely"

Whatever the case, we need the sure Word of God to guide us. Psalm 19 is a reminder that the Bible can save us a lot of heartache by giving us the ability to discern situations with godly wisdom and make God-honoring choices.

It's easy to get frustrated with a child or someone else who won't listen to you, even though you know the person is headed for trouble because you can see further down the road. When another person is intent on making a bad choice, sometimes you have to step aside and let that person learn a hard lesson, especially if the person is a young adult. You can try to advise and warn of the consequences. When I was about to do something my father thought was foolish, he would lay on me that old line that every kid in my generation knows so well: "Use your head for something besides a hat rack." In other words, think about what you're doing, because you're about to mess up.

I love the action and adventure of the Indiana Jones films.

In the third film Dr. Jones was on a search for the Holy Grail, which was supposed to be the cup that Christ drank from at the Last Supper.

When Jones finally tracked down the Grail's location, he found himself in a room with many cups, not knowing which one was the right cup. Unfortunately, the bad guys were also after the cup, and the head bad guy was in the room with Jones. And since the villain had a gun, he got to choose first. The old knight guarding the cups warned the bad guy, "Choose wisely, because if you choose wrong, there are consequences."

You knew this character was going to make a bad choice, of course, and he did—going for a fancy cup that would befit a king. But when he drank from it, he began to melt away right in front of our eyes.

Indiana Jones watched this and realized that a wrong choice meant death. So he began to analyze the situation as he looked over the cups. He remembered that Jesus was a carpenter, so He would likely have had a wooden cup. There was only one wooden cup among the group, so Jones drank from it and was proved right. He also used some of the water from it to heal his father, who had been shot by the bad guy. The cup of cursing to the foolish villain became a cup of blessing to Indiana Jones when he got his thinking straight and chose wisely.

The Bible says there are only two cups in the world, "the cup of the Lord and the cup of demons" (1 Corinthians 10:21), and we cannot drink from both of them. If we choose foolishly, we drink from the bitter cup of the devil. But when we choose wisely, we drink in blessings. God's Word gives us the ability to be wise not in our own eyes, but in the Lord's eyes.

THE BIBLE GIVES US
THE DETAILS OF GOD'S WILL

The third of the psalmist's six declarations in Psalm 19 about Scripture is also packed with good stuff. "The precepts of the Lord are right, rejoicing the heart" (v. 8a). Here David described the Bible using a word that means the particulars of divine instruction.

Sometimes God states explicitly what He does and does not want us to do, while at other times He gives us general principles that apply to a multitude of situations. Both are designed to govern our character and conduct, and both are equally authoritative. God's precepts just spell out things in more detail so that we can live a well-ordered life.

God's Precepts Are Always on Target

One example of a biblical precept is in Proverbs 6:1–5, where we are told not to become "surety," or what we would call a cosigner, for another person's debts. The reason is obvious: If the borrower defaults on the debt, we will be left holding the note and the debt. God's Word tells us by way of principle to be wise in how we handle our finances, but Proverbs 6 gets down to a specific case of avoiding the trap of guaranteeing someone else's debts.

The great thing about the Lord's precepts is that they are always "right," or on target. They never miss the mark. This word in Hebrew means to show someone the correct path, the right way, the road he or she ought to take. Now in the case of avoiding surety, most folk would agree that this is the right thing to do because the risks of taking on another person's debts are enormous. In fact, Proverbs 6 advises the person who has done this not to allow himself any rest until he gets out of that mess.

But God's precepts are right even when nobody else agrees. If the Bible says one thing and everybody else is saying another thing, then everybody else is wrong. The gospel is "foolishness" to the unsaved world (1 Corinthians 1:21), but it is the right path to take. Jesus spoke about two roads, the broad road that is crowded but leads to destruction, and the narrow road that has plenty of room because there are so few people on it (see Matthew 7:13–14). Don't be impressed because your friends are on the broad road. Everybody wants to be on that road because it looks like the way to go. But joy is found on the narrow road with Christ.

The Word of the Lord is a pathfinder. It is the perfect document for people who don't know what to do or which way to turn. It is better to be simple in the world's eyes and need the Word than to be brilliant and think you don't need it.

There Is Joy in Following Jesus

When you obey God's precepts, they rejoice your heart. When you follow the biblically prescribed path, you will be happy you took that road.

How do you know when you're on the right path, especially when everyone else seems to be going the other way? You know the path is right cognitively when it is the path that the Bible prescribes. But you know you are on the right path experientially when you have God's indescribable joy in the midst of the journey, no matter how difficult or painful.

It's like a woman delivering her baby. It's painful, but she knows the pain will produce joy when her baby is placed in her arms. The Word of God operating in the life of the believer will bring joy and rejoicing even when the way is painful.

THE BIBLE GIVES US COMMANDS TO ENLIGHTEN US

There is more good news in Psalm 19, because the Word tells us, "The commandment of the Lord is pure, enlightening the eyes" (v. 8b). This statement expresses the fact that the Bible's teachings are divine mandates, which means they are not optional. God is not writing down suggestions for us to consider. Most people think the Bible contains ten commandments, but here David described all of God's revelation as a commandment that is binding on us.

God isn't the only one looking for our obedience. Many other people want us to take their words seriously and obey what they tell us. How many times did your parents or teachers say to you as a child, "Did you hear what I said?" What they meant was, "Are you going to do what I said or not?"

The trouble with obeying others is that if you aren't careful whom you obey, it can lead to disaster, because people's commands are not pure. The world heard again and again this pathetic defense from Nazi leaders on trial in Nuremberg for killing Jews in World War II: "I was only following orders." Some also tried to argue that as soldiers, they had been trained to follow their commanders' orders and they saw this as their first duty no matter what they were told to do.

The Nazi horror is one of the worst examples of impure human commands that are not fit to be followed. But God's commandments are free of all contamination. Following them will enlighten our eyes and help remove the impurities from our hearts so we can see things clearly.

The opposite of having our eyes enlightened is to have them darkened or blinded. God blinds the eyes and hearts of those who refuse to listen to or obey Him. Jesus prayed in Matthew 11:25, "I praise You, Father, Lord of heaven and earth, that You have hidden these things from the wise and intelligent and have revealed them to infants." The intelligent here are those who are wise in their own eyes and don't feel they need God's Word to enlighten them. But people who are dependent on God get to see life in the blazing light and truth of His Word.

THE BIBLE WILL ENDURE FOREVER

We have two more statements about God's transforming Word to consider from Psalm 19, and they just keep getting better. Beginning in verse 9 we read, "The fear of the Lord is clean, enduring forever."

The word *clean* is similar to pure in that it speaks of an absence of impurity or defilement. God conveys His truth without flaw or blemish. Psalm 12:6 declares, "The words of the Lord are pure words . . . refined seven times."

The fear of the Lord is the reverential fear or awe that the Bible inspires in the hearts of those who love Him and seek to live by His commandments and precepts. The fear of God will last forever, because even when we are in heaven with Jesus, God will not lose any of His majesty, and we will not lose the awe in which He wants us to hold Him. In fact, our awe of the Lord will be infinitely increased when we are with Him in His uninterrupted, holy presence.

As the pure expression of God's heart and mind, the Bible will also last forever. "Forever, O Lord, Your word is settled in heaven" (Psalm 119:89). The Bible is permanent and always relevant. It will never go out of date or out of print.

We have talked about the permanence and never-ending popularity of the Bible. Instead of going out of print, the Bible keeps getting translated into more and more languages.

People dedicate their entire lives to translating the Bible into the languages of obscure or forgotten tribes whose members may only number in the hundreds or thousands. Why? Because these translators are convinced that the Bible is the revelation of God that alone tells us how to be saved, and that when all else of earth is gone, God's Word will remain. It was interesting to study philosophy in college and learn about the worldviews of great thinkers. Many of their ideas have been refined, replaced, or discarded altogether. But the Bible gives us the only worldview, and the only heaven view, that will last forever.

THE BIBLE REVEALS GOD'S RIGHTEOUSNESS

Last certainly does not mean least in the case of Psalm 19:7–9, because the last of David's six declarations about the Word of God is also great: "The judgments of the Lord are true; they are righteous altogether" (v. 9b). Judgments refer to the ordinances or divine verdicts issued from the bench of the Supreme Judge of the earth. The Bible is our infallible standard for judging all of life's situations. God's Word produces righteousness in the life of the believer

who seeks to live by it. Because the Bible is the unadulterated truth
of God, you become right with God when you apply it.

God's Word Is Surpassing in Its Value

The remaining verses of Psalm 19 may be read as expanding this
final statement about God's Word as His judgments. But more likely
they refer to all that David has said in the previous section about
the Bible and its value. But whatever the case, let's look at them in
closing because they answer an important, if unspoken, question:
If the Bible is this incredible and sufficient for all of our needs, what
priority should it have in our lives?

The psalmist spoke to this, and he didn't stutter. The words of
God are "more desirable than gold, yes, than much fine gold" (v. 10a).
It would be news to many people in our culture that there is something more important than money. I would like to think that we as
believers know that, but we unfortunately don't always act like we
know it.

The first time some people realize there are more important
things in life than money is on their deathbed. That's when they want
a Bible or someone who can tell them what life and death are all
about.

When legendary New York Yankees center fielder Mickey Mantle found out in a Dallas hospital that he was dying of a rapidly
spreading form of cancer, a spiritual drama began to unfold that
no one knew about until Mantle's funeral, when his former team-
mate Bobby Richardson told the story.

Mantle had always been afraid to talk about religion, but he knew
the end was near. So he called for his close friend Richardson, a godly
believer who had had an impeccable testimony among his Yankee
teammates. Richardson came to Dallas and shared the gospel with
Mickey Mantle on a Thursday. Mantle received Christ as his Savior,
and when Richardson asked him how he knew he was going to
heaven, Mantle weakly quoted John 3:16 with a big smile on his face.
He died a few days later on Sunday morning. No amount of gold

could have substituted for the gift of eternal life Mickey Mantle received on his deathbed.

Paul knew the surpassing value of the Scriptures. When he was in prison, he asked Timothy to bring his "parchments" (2 Timothy 4:13), his copies of the Old Testament. Paul knew that in his situation, he needed a word from God. The Word is more precious than your paycheck or anything your paycheck can buy, which means anything this world offers.

God's Word Is Sweet in Its Effect

Psalm 19:10 also says the Word of God is "sweeter also than honey and the drippings of the honeycomb." That means it is better than any dessert you can dream of. Have you ever read a passage that became sweet to you? There's nothing else like it. That's why the Bible invites us, "O taste and see that the Lord is good" (Psalm 34:8).

We are not talking about just reading the Bible, but about tasting and savoring what God has said. There's a big difference between reading about a kiss and kissing your sweetheart. The dictionary may accurately describe kissing as an expression of affection that involves two pairs of lips coming into contact with each other. But that doesn't do anything for me. I want love I can feel.

God wants you to taste and savor His Word. For David, the Word was something to be experienced as well as to be known. The Bible is true, but you want more than just the facts of Scripture. You want the reality of it. You want the Bible to take on life, which is the ministry of the Holy Spirit who gives life to the words on the page in front of you. And when that happens, the Scripture will become flavorful to you.

God's Word Is Powerful in Its Protection

In verses 11–13 of Psalm 19, the psalmist continued with a tribute to the Bible's ability to protect believers from sin of every kind. These include "hidden faults" (v. 12), those deep-down flaws we may not always be aware of that can trip us up, and "presumptuous sins" (v. 13), those we plan and deliberately commit. David's goal in all this was to be "blameless" and "acquitted of great transgression."

The psalm closes with a great prayer that expressed David's desire to respond properly to the wonderful truth that God's Word was all he would ever need. "Let the words of my mouth and the meditation of my heart be acceptable in Your sight, O Lord, my rock and my Redeemer" (v. 14).

God's Word is sufficient for every area of life. All the ingredients you need to be acceptable to God are there in the Scripture. You don't have to mess with the recipe. Just dig in and enjoy it.

You may remember an old commercial for Prego spaghetti sauce. A man comes into the kitchen where his wife is making spaghetti. He looks at the sauce on the stove and asks, "Where are the tomatoes?" His wife answers, "They're in there."

Then he asks if the sauce has onions, and again she says, "They're in there." This goes on a few more times as the man asks about various ingredients and the wife says each time, "They're in there." Then we find out the reason this sauce is so comprehensive is that it's Prego.

Well, God's Word has it all in there too. If your life is falling apart, the help you need is already in the Word. You say, "I'm worried. Does God have a word for me?" Yes, it's in there. "I don't know how I am going to pay my bills." It's in there. "I just found out I have cancer." It's in there.

Whatever you need, it's in there, because the Bible is sufficient to address every need you will ever have.

THE COMMUNICATION OF GOD'S WORD

THE COMMUNICATION OF GOD'S WORD

6
THE REVELATION OF THE BIBLE

I love visiting New York and taking in all the sights and sounds of that great city. Every opportunity I have to go to New York is exciting to me, because the place is pulsating with life twenty-four hours a day.

One of the things I like to do when I'm in New York is take in a musical or drama of some sort on Broadway. There is something about live theater with all the characters and the action happening right in front of you that is fascinating to watch. Many of these performances are sold out, and there is usually a large crowd in the theater. You can hear a lot of small talk, but can also feel a tremendous sense of anticipation and excitement in the air as the audience waits for the curtains to rise and the play to begin.

I feel this sense of excitement too, for I know that when the curtains go up there is going to be a revelation. Something special that has been hidden from our view and understanding until that moment is about to be made manifest. A story is about to unfold before us, and I know it is going to be good.

Or to put it another way, when the curtains go up it's show time! There is something about this act of revealing what has been hidden that makes people quit talking and listen, and those who don't get quiet and pay attention are told, "Shhhh! The show is about to begin!"

God also had a great drama that He wanted to present to the human race, and when His time was right He raised the curtains and unveiled what had not been known before. The biblical word for this unveiling or curtain-raising is "revelation," or apocalypse. This latter word is simply a transliteration of the Greek term that means "revelation." It is the title of the last book in the Bible, which we could also call the final act in God's great cosmic drama of sin and redemption.

In this section of the book I want to consider five aspects of the Bible that have to do with God's once-only delivery of His Word to us, and His ongoing work in aiding our understanding and application of it. God's revelation has been recorded and preserved for us in written verbal form, but when it was first revealed to its authors and other "actors," a good portion of the Bible was also accompanied by a visual display.

This interplay between the visual and verbal aspects of revelation helps to give us a working definition of this doctrine of Scripture. Revelation is the supernatural work of God whereby He makes known, either by verbal disclosure or visible display, that which was previously unknown or hidden. God does this so that we might come to know the truth He wants us to know—and which we desperately need to know in order to be rightly related to Him—but which we could never discover on our own apart from Him.

GOD HAS CHOSEN
TO MAKE HIMSELF KNOWN TO US

It is critically important that you grasp how utterly and completely dependent we were upon God's grace to reveal Himself to us.

Remember, general revelation in nature is enough to condemn the one who ignores it and doesn't seek God.

God Is Higher than We Can Conceive

Without God's self-disclosure to us in His Word, we would be hopelessly lost. This is true not only because God is infinitely higher than anything or anyone we can imagine, but also because if God had not lifted the curtain of heaven and revealed Himself, there would have been no divine story and no salvation for lost sinners like us.

One of the dramas that emerged from the San Francisco earthquake of 1989 illustrates how desperately we need God to reveal Himself to us. The extensive television coverage of this quake allowed us to see things we would not ordinarily have seen. Many tragic scenes played out before us, one of which was the car that accidentally turned in the wrong direction on the Golden Gate Bridge and suddenly plunged between two sections of the roadbed that had broken apart. You may remember that others who knew the danger desperately signaled the driver to stop, but the car went on ahead and the driver was killed.

This is exactly the danger we are in without God's self-disclosure. We would have had no idea of the danger and destruction into which we were headed. You can read Isaiah 55:8–9 again to refresh yourself on how God and His thoughts are totally above and apart from us and our thoughts.

Paul made a strong statement of this truth as he concluded a magnificent section in Romans 9–11 about God's dealings with Israel: "Oh, the depth of the riches both of the wisdom and knowledge of God! How unsearchable are His judgments and unfathomable His ways! For who has known the mind of the Lord, or who became His counselor?" (Romans 11:33–34).

The fact is that God is not like us. He doesn't think or operate the way we do. Older theologians used to refer to God as the "Wholly Other." Since this is true, God has to make sense of Himself for us.

We can't figure Him out, because our only reference point for trying to understand God is ourselves.

This is why whenever people try to concoct their own view of God, they will always come up with an idol or some other unworthy representation of God. Our finite minds can only conceive of that which is finite.

Most of us can't even figure out the spouse we have been living with for twenty, thirty, or forty or more years. Scientists have been trying for centuries to explain how the universe came into being, and they haven't arrived at it yet because they usually begin by removing God from the formula. God is as far removed from our experience as the heavens are removed from the earth.

Sin Darkens Our Ability to Comprehend God

There is another reason that God must reveal Himself in order for us to know Him. Ephesians 4:18 says that our hearts have been "darkened" by the plague of sin. This is true of our minds as well. Sin has messed up our thinking so badly it's as if we are wearing blinders that limit our spiritual perception and ability to understand God. Besides, our first inclination as sinners is to hide from God in an attempt to keep Him from knowing us. It was only after Adam and Eve had sinned that they tried to hide from God when He came to take His daily walk with them in the garden (see Genesis 3:8).

Before this, they had walked with God in Eden, which suggests they had an intimate relationship with Him. That relationship changed drastically when Adam and Eve sinned. And ever since, people have been blinded to the reality of God by their sin and trying their best to hide from Him.

GENERAL REVELATION
SHOWS GOD'S EXISTENCE AND POWER

We're talking about revelation in broader terms than just the Bible because it's important to see where the Scripture fits in God's ages-long, unfolding plan to reveal Himself to the human race. Paul said that God "did not leave Himself without witness" (Acts 14:17).

Paul made this statement during his sermon to the pagan people of Lystra, and it refers to God's witness in nature through the general revelation He gives to all men. But everything God did to disclose Himself to us is His witness.

God Has Left Himself a Witness in Nature

In our discussion of general revelation in the previous chapter, we learned that God has written the message of His existence with an unmistakable hand in the heavens above and the world around, so that all men have a clear picture that He exists. Creation manifests the reality of God even without words (see Psalm 19:3).

In addition to its theaters, New York City also has many museums where you can view the work of great artists. The last time I checked, no museum was displaying a beautiful work of art and saying that it had come into being without a master's hand. Even those works of art whose authorship is unknown or in doubt are assumed to be the creation of some artist. And in fact, great effort is often expended to track down and identify the author of a masterpiece so he or she can receive the honor due.

It's amazing that God doesn't even get the respect the world gives to a good painter. But look at the canvas He has painted on. Every time you say, "What a beautiful day this is," you are saying, "What a great artist God is. Can He ever paint!" Folks who think this universe is the work of some anonymous artist who forgot to sign his work—or even worse, the result of blind forces with no guiding hand—need to wake up and read the witness of creation. The Bible says it takes a fool to deny the existence of God.

People Have No Excuse

People can walk through a museum, view its works of art, realize that great masters created them, and then walk out of the building without having to make any decisions about the way they are living. But that's not true of God's revelation in nature. It is clear enough that God can demand that people do something about it.

This was the thrust of Paul's famous message in Acts 17:22–31 to the idolatrous Greeks in Athens when he saw them ignorantly worshiping an "unknown God." Paul was deeply disturbed by their foolish ideas, and he used God's witness in nature to argue that they needed to seek the true God in repentance. I want to note some of the highlights of that message, and then we'll deal with special revelation.

Paul's argument to these idol worshipers followed this line of reasoning. First, the Creator God who made everything is not at all like us in that He cannot be reduced to living in man-made temples, nor does He need anything from us (Acts 17:24–25). Not only that, but He cannot be represented by man-made images of gold, silver, or stone (v. 29).

Second, this God who made the world and everything in it gave men His witness in nature in order that "they might grope for Him and find Him" (v. 27). I love the way Paul stated the goal of general revelation: "Therefore having overlooked the times of ignorance, God is now declaring to men that all people everywhere should repent" (v. 30).

Third, the reason people need to seek God in repentance is that He is going to convene a court of judgment someday and hold them accountable for their unbelief (v. 31).

That's an outline any preacher can work with! No man or woman will be able to stand before God and say, "You didn't give me enough data to believe in You." The Bible says that all alike are "without excuse" before God (Romans 1:20). Like a gigantic billboard staring at us on the highway, creation is a witness to God's glory that is plain to everybody. People who ignore it do so at their own peril.

Special Revelation Shows God's Character

Suppose you attend a great orchestra concert with thousands of other people. Everybody in the audience gets to see the performers on stage at a distance and hear the beautiful music they create, but the general audience can't interact with the musicians and conductor or have personal interaction with them.

But in addition to your ticket, you also have a backstage pass that allows you to go behind the scenes and meet the performers and the composers of the evening's music. You learn their names and all about their families, hear them explain how the musical compositions you have just enjoyed came into being, and learn in detail about the works they are writing now and their plans for future concerts. Your backstage pass as opposed to just a general admission ticket is the difference between general and special revelation. Special revelation takes us from being in the "audience" at God's creation to intimate, personal fellowship and interaction with Him.

Here's another way to compare these two aspects of God's self-disclosure. One of the television programs that kids watched every week when I was growing up was *The Lone Ranger.* He was a mysterious masked man who would show up in a town with his faithful companion, Tonto, to help the local sheriff bring the bad guys to justice.

The town's sheriff didn't know exactly who this masked stranger was or where he came from, and in many episodes the sheriff expressed doubt that anyone wearing a mask could be on the side of the law. But the Lone Ranger assured the lawman that he had nothing to fear from his mask, and, as the show went on, the Lone Ranger demonstrated to the sheriff that he was someone who could be trusted. The sheriff liked what he saw and heard, and sure enough the Lone Ranger and Tonto would deliver the crooks into his hands and restore peace to the town.

The program always ended with the sheriff or one of the other locals asking, "Who was that masked man?" as the duo rode out of town in a cloud of dust. Someone else standing there always answered, "Why, don't you know? He's the Lone Ranger!" I used to love the look of awe and respect the sheriff would always get on his face as the identity of the mysterious stranger was revealed to him and he realized he had been in the presence of the famous Lone Ranger.

What happened on an episode of *The Long Ranger* is basically what happens when we move from general to special revelation. When we see what God has done in nature, we should want to know more about Him. We should be asking, "Who is this Being that is so awesome and powerful He can make all of this, and what is He like?" This is the question that is answered by special revelation, which takes up where general revelation ends. Special revelation has come to us in two forms we can see and read and understand— Jesus, the Son of God, and the Bible, the written Word of God.

People often refer to Jesus and the Bible as the living and the written Word. But both are actually the living Word, because the Bible is "living and active" (Hebrews 4:12). So it would be more biblically and theologically accurate to say that the Bible is the living written Word of God, and Jesus is the living incarnate Word of God—referring to Jesus' coming to earth when "the Word became flesh, and dwelt among us" (John 1:14).

These two revelations agree as one, for the written Word testifies to the truthfulness of Jesus, and Jesus testifies to the truthfulness of the written Word. Jesus is the visible display of God, and the Bible is the verbal display of God. Both are heaven's answer to the question: Who is this God of creation, and what is He like? Let's consider Jesus first.

God Has Revealed Himself in the Person of Christ

The apostle John opened his Gospel by teaching us that Jesus is the eternal God who came down from heaven to take on a body and live among us. John called Jesus "the Word" (1:1) because He is the perfect expression of God. Jesus is also the Word because He came to deliver God's message.

The author of Hebrews opened his letter with a tremendous explanation of Jesus' uniqueness: "God, after He spoke long ago to the fathers in the prophets in many portions and in many ways, in these last days has spoken to us in His Son, whom He appointed heir of all things, through whom also He made the world. And He is the radiance of His glory and the exact representation of His nature, and upholds all things by the word of His power" (vv. 1–3a).

In the Old Testament, God spoke to the patriarchs and prophets in many ways besides through His words. These include fire, displays in nature, visions, dreams—and once even through a donkey (see Numbers 22:28–30). But all of these were small events leading to the main event when God spoke by His Son.

Hebrews 1:1–3 makes the same basic point as John 1, which is that God sent His one and only Son to demonstrate who He is and what He is like by bringing us His final and climactic message. Jesus Christ came to give us the details about God—doing so by His life, death, and resurrection, which were visual, and by His teachings, which were verbal.

God Has Revealed Himself in the Pages of His Word

The written Word of God is the other aspect of God's self-revelation to us. The Bible is the verbal manifestation of God, His "authorized autobiography" by which we get to know Him personally. Since Jesus is no ordinary man but the invisible God supernaturally made visible to us, His Word is no ordinary book but the supernatural Word of God to us.

Jesus told the people of His day that they searched the Scriptures in hopes of finding eternal life. There's nothing wrong with that, because the Bible is the Word of eternal life. But then Jesus said, "It is these that testify about Me; and you are unwilling to come to Me so that you may have life" (John 5:39–40). What Jesus was saying is that there is no contradiction or disconnect between Him as the incarnate Son of God and the Scriptures as the Word of God. They both convey the same message.

Let me say it again. There is no such thing as people claiming that they follow Jesus but don't necessarily believe the Bible. Every parent knows how good children are at playing the parents against each other. They get permission to do something from the parent who is more likely to give it, and then use that when the other parent says no. "But Daddy said we could!" "Mama said it was OK!" That's why it is so important for parents to be on the same page, so the kids get the same message from Daddy and Mama on the important issues.

Jesus and the Bible speak the same message from God. Jesus said on another occasion, "It is the Spirit who gives life; the flesh profits nothing; the words that I have spoken to you are spirit and are life" (John 6:63). The Bible's words are the living words of the living God.

It's also important to mention that the moment the last word of the last book of the Bible was recorded under the Holy Spirit's inspiration, God's revelation was completed. There is no "second" or "expanded" edition of the Bible. We'll deal with this important issue in an upcoming chapter on the canon of Scripture, or how the books of the Bible were chosen to be included in the sacred text before it was closed. Suffice it to say here that the Bible is the complete Word of God to us.

One of the traits of almost every cult is the claim to have extra-biblical revelation from God that supposedly explains the Bible more fully, or more often contradicts what the Bible teaches. But those claims are absolutely, categorically false. God illumines Scripture to us, but He has said His final Word in the Person of Jesus, as Hebrews 1:1–3 says so eloquently. Be careful of folk who claim that God told them something He hasn't told anyone else in the two-thousand-year history of the church. If it isn't in the Bible, it is not God's Word.

GOD'S WORD HOLDS
MANY VALUABLE BENEFITS FOR US

This is another one of those topics that could fill a book, but I want to show you several benefits that the Bible provides for your encouragement as we wrap up the discussion on the Scripture as God's revelation, or self-disclosure, to us.

God's Word Teaches Us to Worship God

The Bible reveals the priority that worship should have in our lives and teaches us how to worship properly. "Ascribe to the Lord the glory due to His name; worship the Lord in holy array" declares the psalmist (Psalm 29:2). Psalm 89:5–7 says that God's creation and His holy angels praise and fear Him. We ought to be doing the same because He redeemed us.

I would encourage you to get a Bible concordance if you don't already have one. A concordance lists every word in the Bible and gives the reference, so you can trace a thought or concept through the entire Scripture. If you want to revolutionize and energize your worship, start tracing words like "worship," "praise," and "glorify" through the Bible and see what God has said about the kind of worship He desires. We know He is seeking worshipers because Jesus said so (see John 4:23).

God didn't give us the Bible to make us smart, but to make us holy and give us an incurable appetite to know and worship Him. I always think of the biblical scholars in Jerusalem who knew the answer to the Magi's question when they came to King Herod looking for the baby "who has been born King of the Jews" (Matthew 2:2).

Herod called together these experts in the Old Testament and asked them where this new King had been born. These men knew their Bible and answered right away, "In Bethlehem of Judea," and then proceeded to quote the prophecy of Micah 5:2 (Matthew 2:5–6).

The Magi went on to Bethlehem, about five miles away, found Jesus, and worshiped Him (v. 11). But wait a minute. Where were the Bible scholars who told the Magi where Jesus could be found? They had the right biblical information, but they didn't bother to make the trip to Bethlehem to find out if this child was in fact their Messiah.

God did not give you the Bible so you can tell folk what you know. He gave you the Bible so you would take the trip to visit the Savior and worship Almighty God. God has revealed Himself so that we can come to know and worship the living God in all of His majesty and holiness.

God's Word Gives Us a Perfect Standard

Another benefit of God's revelation is that it gives us a completely reliable standard by which to assess and measure divine reality. The Bible is a new pair of glasses through which God wants us to look at Him and all of life.

Many people think it's cool to say, "I'm a natural man." Well, from God's perspective it isn't. The Bible says, "A natural man does not accept the things of the Spirit of God, for they are foolishness to him; and he cannot understand them, because they are spiritually appraised" (1 Corinthians 2:14).

Paul continued, "But he who is spiritual appraises all things, yet he himself is appraised by no one. For who has known the mind of the Lord, that he will instruct Him? But we have the mind of Christ" (vv. 15–16). The spiritual person sees everything from a different perspective because he appraises or evaluates life from God's perspective.

Having "the mind of Christ" tells us that when we judge everything by the standard of God's Word, we are looking at things the way Jesus would look at them. Now we don't do that perfectly, of course, but the only way to get God's view on life is to look at it through the lens of His Word. The mind of Christ, as revealed in the Scripture, gives us the ability to see the invisible realm through the eyes of faith. And that divine perspective changes everything.

God's Word Reveals His Ways and Means

The U.S. Congress has a standing committee known as "Ways and Means." Somebody said that what Congress needs is a "Ways and Mean It" committee, but that's another story.

God has His ways and means too, and He means every word of what He says. The Bible reveals God's ways and means, or His purposes, so that we can know the right path to take. Proverbs 14:12 is a very sobering verse to me: "There is a way which seems right to a man, but its end is the way of death." In other words, use your human logic alone to chart the course of your life, and it will eventually take you down a path that's headed straight into hell. The best example of this I can think of is Israel under the judges, a dark and disastrous period when "everyone did what was right in his own eyes" (Judges 21:25).

The remedy to keep us from making this kind of mess out of our lives is also found in the proverbs: "Trust in the Lord with all your heart and do not lean on your own understanding. In all your ways acknowledge Him, and He will make your paths straight" (Proverbs 3:5–6). God doesn't want us coming to crucial crossroads in our lives with nothing to guide us but human opinions and ideas. He wants us to know His ways.

God's Word Fixes Our Broken Lives

God also reveals Himself in His Word in order to fix what is broken in our lives. James 1:21 says, "Putting aside all filthiness and all that remains of wickedness, in humility receive the word implanted, which is able to save your souls."

That word *save* means more than simply justification or pardon from sin. It refers to making whole whatever is broken or fouled up within us. The way this works is something like taking your broken car to the dealership for repairs. The mechanics there have sophisticated diagnostic tools they can use to pinpoint what is wrong and precision repair tools to correct the problem that is keeping your car from performing up to the maker's specifications.

The Word of God is both the powerful diagnostic tool God uses to pinpoint what is broken in our lives and the repair tool He uses to fix it so we can perform up to our divine Maker's specifications. If you will take the Bible to heart and orient all of life to it, God will use His Word not only to fix what is broken but also to deliver you from future disasters, because the Bible is not just a book. It is the living and active revelation of God.

7
THE INSPIRATION OF THE BIBLE

Most people know what it's like to experience a moment of inspiration when you come up with a really good idea, or the words of a poem or song or some other piece of creative work just seem to flow from you.

But there is another level of inspiration that the vast majority of us will never know. I'm thinking of examples like the German-born composer, George Frederick Handel. Handel was said to be at a low point in his career in 1741 when he began writing his world-famous oratorio known as *Messiah*. Among other problems, Handel was suffering from partial paralysis on his left side as the result of a stroke.

But when the great composer began writing *Messiah*, Handel experienced an incredible rush of inspiration that allowed him to overcome these obstacles and finish this majestic work in the unbelievable span of just twenty-one days.

Of course, inspiration involves a lot more than just time. Another classic example of human inspiration is the Italian artist Michelangelo, who was commissioned by Pope Julius II in 1508 to repaint the ceiling of the Sistine Chapel. Michelangelo worked on that masterpiece from 1508 to 1512. He was later commissioned to paint the *Last Judgement* over the Sistine's altar. Michelangelo worked on this painting from 1535 to 1541.

If you were to ask people on the street for their definition of inspiration, most would probably talk about that feeling of exaltation, of being carried or lifted up, that a person gets when his spirit is raised to a higher level. Other people might use words like encouragement, motivation, or stimulation to describe the experience of being inspired. And they might use the work of geniuses like Handel or Michelangelo to illustrate what it means to be truly inspired.

It's interesting that two dictionaries from two different but authoritative publishers show a marked difference in the way the word *inspiration* is defined. One dictionary's first definition is a "divine influence" that a person receives that allows him to "receive and communicate sacred revelation." The second dictionary lists this aspect of inspiration as its last definition and begins with the basic definition of inspiration as the act of breathing in air, or inhaling. This physical meaning is not far removed from the emotional or spiritual side of inspiration, as we will see.

When discussing what inspiration means, more theologically aware people may even cite the Bible as an example of inspiration. The Bible is certainly inspired, but not in the way that any other work has ever been inspired before, or ever will be again. Inspiration takes on a unique meaning when applied to God's Word.

The Greek word translated "inspired" (2 Timothy 3:16) is *theophneustos,* which means "God-breathed." It is a compound word made up of the words for God and breath or spirit. The *New International Version* translates this word literally when it says, "All Scripture is God-breathed." Thus inspiration is the breath of God as He breathes out His Word. Scripture came from God as words come from the mouth of a person who is speaking (see Romans 3:2; 16:25).

Thus the Bible does not simply contain the Word of God; it *is* the very words of God. The Holy Spirit inspired His chosen men to write the Bible, and the result is the only Book in history that flawlessly communicates God's Word and will to man.

With this information, let's put together a biblical definition of inspiration and then consider its process and its product. The doctrine of inspiration refers to the process by which God oversaw the composition of Scripture through its authors in such a way that they recorded its message exactly the way God wanted it recorded, without error or omission. Inspiration guarantees that God's revelation, that which He disclosed concerning Himself, has come to us without contamination.

THE PROCESS OF INSPIRATION

The reason we can study truths like the inspiration of the Bible is that, unlike all other so-called gods, our God speaks. One appropriate name or title for the true and living God is "the God who speaks."

The psalmist said of idols that are the work of human hands, "They have mouths, but they cannot speak" (Psalm 115:5). The prophets often mocked the impotence and silence of the false gods that the nations around Israel, and ultimately Israel herself, came to trust in. "Like a scarecrow in a cucumber field are they, and they cannot speak" (Jeremiah 10:5). No god but our great God has anything to say. In the Old Testament alone, you will encounter the phrase, "Thus saith the Lord," or some derivative thereof, more than three thousand times.

Inspiration Applies to the Words of the Bible

The doctrine of inspiration addresses the relationship between the God who speaks and the human writers who recorded what the God who speaks had to say. The place where God's words were written and collected is the Bible. Again, it is critically important that we understand that inspiration is the process by which "men moved by the Holy Spirit spoke from God" (2 Peter 1:21). Over and over again, the authors of Scripture declared their message to be the Word of God given through them to their readers, not just their best thoughts about God. And because their message was from God, it carried His authority.

For example, consider what Paul wrote to the church at Corinth, which was full of proud people and those who challenged the apostle's authority. Speaking of this church's misuse of the gift of tongues and his correction for this abuse, Paul said, "If anyone thinks he is a prophet or spiritual, let him recognize that the things which I write to you are the Lord's commandment" (1 Corinthians 14:37).

And by the way, when the prophets and apostles presented the Word of God to His people, they didn't do so with any hesitation, hemming and hawing, or apology. In the very next verse, Paul wrote, "But if anyone does not recognize this, he is not recognized" (v. 38). In other words, God's Word came with His authority because He inspired it. To set aside or ignore the Word was to be set aside by God.

I could say a lot more about this, but for now notice the thrust of Paul's argument. He was bold enough to say that when the Corinthians read his letter, they were reading a letter written by the hand of God as surely as if it had come sealed and addressed straight from heaven. The doctrine of inspiration means that every word in the original autographs or manuscripts of Scripture is from God. He didn't waste any words or leave out anything He wanted to say, and neither did the Bible's writers toss in their own ideas here and there.

Evangelicals are often accused of being nitpicky or narrow in our view of Scripture. Well, so be it if that's the charge. But insisting on the inspiration of the entire Bible is important because anything less is like leaving the barn door open just a few inches. When you do that, one of the animals inside will inevitably come up to the door and push against it to see if it really is unlatched. Pretty soon the door will be wide-open and all the animals will get out.

Leaving the door open to the possibility that any or some of the words of Scripture are not inspired of God is giving away the whole farm, so to speak. That's why the statement that the Bible *contains* the Word of God is incorrect. This suggests that the Bible contains other words that are not from God. The Bible *is,* not merely contains, the Word of God.

Inspiration Is the Breath of God as He Speaks

I said earlier that the basic definition of inspiration as the act of breathing in air is related to the biblical use of this word to describe God's "breathing out" of His Word.

This was as much a creative act on God's part as when He breathed the "breath of life" into Adam's nostrils and he came alive (Genesis 2:7). What happened when God inspired holy men to write the Bible is that they were carried along, as it were, by God's breath. That is, they were inspired or lifted up by God. I'll have more to say about this later because there is another biblical word for this process that is very picturesque and interesting.

When Paul said that all Scripture is God-breathed, he was asserting that the Scripture came from God's mouth the way a person's breath leaves his body when he speaks. This concept emphasizes the immediacy and directness of God's speaking, rather than just hearing from someone that God said something.

It's the difference between standing in front of your father when he tells you to do something and he asks you, "Did you hear what I said?" and only hearing secondhand that your dad wanted a job done. My father's words had real power and authority with me. When he spoke to me, he expected a response and expected it quickly.

In my home, the same was true for my mother's word. I remember the day we were playing baseball in the alley behind our home in Baltimore. These games were a big deal to the kids in my neighborhood, because we couldn't advance to playing on a field with the older guys until we had proved ourselves in the alley. So I took these games very seriously.

On this particular day, the game was on the line in the bottom of the ninth and I was due to come to bat with a chance to be the hero. But just then my younger brother showed up with this message: "Mama told me to tell you, 'Stop what you are doing and come home right now.'"

You have to understand my thinking at that moment. This was definitely not a "Mama says to come home" situation. I was out there with my boys, and the game was riding on my shoulders. I couldn't just quit and go home, so I told my brother to tell Mama, "I'm coming," which being interpreted meant, "I'll be there as soon as the game is over, however long that takes."

The only problem was that this was not what Mama had said, so when I eventually got home I had to face her in judgment. "You are punished for disobeying me. I told your brother to tell you that I wanted you home immediately. You can't go out in the alley and play for the rest of this week."

To me that was the worst of all punishments, but I knew I didn't have a leg to stand on in protest. My brother had delivered the "authorized version" of my mama's message, and his words carried her authority. So even though her word came through somebody else, I was accountable to obey my mama.

God expects no less from us, for His Word comes to us with great power. I love the way Psalm 147 pictures the power of God's inspired Word: "He sends forth His command to the earth; His word runs very swiftly. . . . He sends forth His word and melts [ice]; He causes His wind to blow and the waters to flow. He declares His words to Jacob, His statutes and His ordinances to Israel" (vv. 15, 18–19).

GOD'S WORDS ARE FOUND IN THE BIBLE

Back in 2 Timothy 3:16, where Paul said all Scripture is inspired by God, the word *Scripture* emphasizes that the words God spoke did not just float away, but were written down. The Greek word is *graphe*, which is a familiar component of many English words. It means a piece of writing. Not only does God affirm again and again in Scripture that He speaks or breathes out His Word (see Deuteron-omy 9:10), but you will also read that these words were recorded by men (Exodus 17:14; Deuteronomy 31:19; Revelation 1:10–11). For example, John writes, "These things I have written unto you" (1 John 5:13).

God is into writing, because the Bible says in Deuteronomy 9:10 that the Ten Commandments were written with "the finger of God." Whenever I read this, I think of the classic Cecil B. DeMille film called *The Ten Commandments,* which is still shown on television every once in a while. When Moses is on the mountain receiving the commandments, this fingerlike bolt of fire comes out of heaven and blazes each commandment into the stone, while Moses looks on in great fear and awe. It's a spectacular scene that reminds the viewer that this is, quite literally, the Word written by God.

Now I want you to notice something else important in 2 Timo-thy 3:16. The verse does not say that the writers of Scripture were inspired, but that what they wrote is inspired. This takes the empha-sis off of questions such as whether the authors of Scripture drew on their own vocabulary to express the thoughts the Holy Spirit gave them, or whether the Spirit simply dictated the Bible to them word by word the way a boss dictates a letter to his secretary.

The fact that each writer's style and vocabulary are different shows that the Spirit drew on the authors' personalities as He revealed the Word to them. But we are not told the details of how the process of inspiration was carried out, because God wants us to know that the finished product is His Word, spoken from His mouth. And the Word is not only God's thoughts, but also His very words that make up those thoughts (see Exodus 4:15; Deuteronomy 4:2).

We can't say it enough. Scripture is the Word, and words, of God. Keeping the emphasis there helps us answer the argument that since human beings wrote the Bible, it is therefore merely a human book. Inspiration assures us that these men, though imperfect and flawed, were guarded from error as they wrote the Scriptures.

The Holy Spirit Is the Agent of Inspiration

The closest we come to a description of the process of inspiration is 2 Peter 1:20–21, where the apostle wrote: "But know this first of all, that no prophecy of Scripture is a matter of one's own interpretation, for no prophecy was ever made by an act of the human will, but *men moved by the Holy Spirit* spoke from God" (italics added). We have the Bible because the Holy Spirit acted in a unique way upon the prophets and apostles, or their assistants, to record God's words.

The word *moved* (*pheromenoi*) is very interesting because it pictures a sailboat on the water with the sail catching the wind and moving or carrying the boat along. The word is used this way in Acts 27:15, where Luke said that when Paul was in the storm on his way to Rome, the wind blew his ship along with such force that the ship had to go wherever the wind wanted it to go.

What wind is to a sailboat, Peter said the Holy Spirit was to the writers of Scripture. The image of the Spirit, who is Himself the wind or the breath of God, moving the biblical writers to record what God wanted fits well with what we said earlier about Scripture coming from God's mouth as His very breath. Just as the strong wind in Acts 27 carried Paul's ship along, so the Spirit carried the writers of Scripture in the direction God wanted them to go.

Again, this does not mean that the Spirit negated or overrode the uniqueness of each author. The Spirit's inspiration of the biblical writers is like the electricity that comes into your home. It serves as the power source for various tools and appliances that are unique in their makeup and in the task they are designed to accomplish. The Spirit inspired the biblical writers to express the Word of God through the uniqueness of their personalities, but He did so in such a way that what they wrote can still be called the words of God.

Jesus made a great promise the night before His crucifixion concerning the Holy Spirit. "The Helper, the Holy Spirit, whom the Father will send in My name, He will teach you all things, and bring to your remembrance all that I said to you" (John 14:26). We can claim this verse as a promise, but it most directly relates to the apostles to whom it was first spoken.

These men could not possibly have remembered everything Jesus said and did. But they didn't have to worry, because Jesus said the Holy Spirit would bring it all back when it came time to write it down. In other words, all that men like Peter, John, and Matthew had to do was keep their sails up and the Holy Spirit would catch them and move them in the right direction.

This sailboat imagery helps us understand the relationship between the human authors of Scripture and God as the divine Author. The wind is the power that moves the boat, but the boat also requires a sail to move. A great verse that speaks to this relationship is Acts 1:16. As Peter addressed the need to replace Judas among the apostles, he began by saying, "Brethren, the Scripture had to be fulfilled, *which the Holy Spirit foretold by the mouth of David* concerning Judas, who became a guide to those who arrested Jesus" (italics added).

According to Peter, the Holy Spirit put His words in the mouth of David so that when David spoke, what came out was called Scripture. When Peter went on to quote from the Psalms (69:25 and 109:8 in Acts 1:20), the apostles in that meeting were hearing God speak even though David had been dead for nine hundred years.

This principle also has application to us today as the people of God. When we gather as the church to hear the Word of God proclaimed, our prayer should be, "Lord, I want to hear from You today through the sermon."

Now don't misunderstand. The pastor is not speaking new revelation, but he is proclaiming the Word that God spoke to His people for our spiritual correction, growth, and benefit. Paul said that the same "all Scripture" that is inspired by God is also "profitable for teaching, for reproof, for correction, for training in righteousness; so that the man of God may be adequate, equipped for every good work" (2 Timothy 3:16–17).

Every Sunday and Wednesday evening, the maintenance crew at our church comes in after the services and cleans up the notes that some people take during a sermon and then leave in the pew or on the floor. A lot of what preachers say gets left on the floor, and that's OK if it's only the words of a human being. But the goal of preaching the Word is that the church might hear the voice of God speaking through the human mouthpiece.

You Need to Keep Your Sails Up!

I want to make another important application before we leave this discussion on the process of inspiration. You and I have spiritual sails too, which the Bible calls "ears" to hear what the Holy Spirit is saying to us. We are not writing Scripture today; God's revelation is complete. But you and I need the Spirit's wisdom and guidance to properly understand and apply the Scriptures to our daily lives.

How does the Holy Spirit lead you to choose which job to take, or which person to marry? You may have several choices, any one of which would be within the boundaries of God's will. The name of a person's future mate is not in the Bible, but the Word of God does say to believers, "Do not be bound together with unbelievers" (2 Corinthians 6:14).

Clear biblical principles like this are part of the "wind" of the Holy Spirit to move you along in the right direction concerning a marriage partner. The same process applies to making other life decisions. God wants to lead you each day by His Holy Spirit, but you have to be ready to hear Him. If you are a Christian and yet you are not experiencing the Spirit's leading, it's because your sail is down. That means it's time to get into your prayer closet and shut the door, and not come out until you have a clear word from God.

The Holy Spirit moves Christians today in the application of divine truth. You do not have to live in ambiguity as a Christian, because you have the Holy Spirit inside of you and His wind is blowing.

THE PRODUCT OF INSPIRATION

We have spent most of our time in this chapter on the process of inspiration, and that is by design. We have already presented arguments and proofs for the inerrancy of Scripture, so I don't need to spend too much time demonstrating that the product of inspiration is exactly what God wanted. But here are several important truths to consider under this heading.

God Still Has His Secrets

The Bible doesn't tell us everything there is to know about God, just what He wants us to know. Deuteronomy 29:29 says, "The secret things belong to the Lord our God, but the things revealed belong to us and to our sons forever, that we may observe all the words of this law." The Bible has everything you need to know to obey and please God.

Don't worry about the stuff you don't know or the questions that are still unanswered. Eternity is going to be filled with new revelation about God, and it will unfold forever because our God is infinite and eternal in His creativity. What we see now is just the beginning of the things God wants to reveal to us. We haven't seen anything yet about the awesome perfections and majesty of God.

We Have a Perfect and Complete Bible

Because of the Holy Spirit's work of overseeing and superintending the inspiration of Scripture, in the Bible we have a perfect and complete text of everything God desired to reveal to men. If this teaching of the care and attention that God gave to every word of Scripture is somewhat new to you, here is a good passage to meditate on: "Every word of God is tested. . . . Do not add to His words or He will reprove you, and you will be proved a liar" (Proverbs 30:5–6). God has weighed and examined every word to get just the ones He wanted. Our job is to explain and teach the Scriptures, not to try to figure out which of its words are inspired and true and which ones aren't. Anybody who says God's Word needs to be improved upon or edited is a liar.

Since God's Word is His perfect revelation, all other words must adjust to His. We can't take the parts we like and discard those parts that don't fit with our preconceived ideas of what God should be like. One reason we have so many incomplete Christians today is that they believe in an incomplete Bible. But all of Scripture must be believed and obeyed.

God's Word Will Last Forever

Not only can we put our faith in every word of Scripture, but we also don't have to worry that the truths and promises of the Word will ever expire. "Heaven and earth will pass away, but My words will not pass away" is our Lord's assurance to us (Matthew 24:35). That milk in your refrigerator has an expiration date on it, after which the guarantee of freshness is over and you are on your own. The company that packaged this milk knows how long it should be good for, based on the nature of milk and the method of processing.

Jesus was saying about the Word, "Based on what My Father and I have put into this product, it is going to last forever." This is why all attempts to destroy the Bible have always failed, even though there have been many throughout history. People have given their lives to make sure that we would have a Bible in our hands, in our own language, because they believed that nothing was more important than making God's eternal Word accessible to all.

This Word from God Meets Our Every Need

I mentioned earlier that 2 Timothy 3:16–17 holds a tremendous "payoff" for those who take God's inspired Word seriously and allow the Holy Spirit to apply it to their lives. The Bible is "profitable" because it is designed to shape and mature us into people God can use to accomplish the work of His kingdom.

There is not a spiritual need you will ever have that is not addressed in Scripture. All of us need "teaching," "reproof," "correction," and "training in righteousness" if we are to become the people God wants us to be. Scripture is sufficient for all of life.

The "teaching" of the Word is what we need to know, the information God has transmitted to us. The Word's "reproof" tells us where we have gone off the path, and it provides "correction" to show us how to make it right. "Training in righteousness" refers to that which we must have to live life as God intended it to be lived. When the Holy Spirit is free to apply the Word of God to our hearts, we will experience the power and delight of being "adequate, equipped for every good work."

Don't let that word *adequate* throw you off. It may convey the idea of barely enough or just so-so in English, but here it means "sufficient to the need." There is nothing God asks you to do that His Word does not give you the tools to accomplish.

8

THE ILLUMINATION OF THE BIBLE

If you talk to enough teachers, you will learn that for many of them the most exciting moment in their day is when a student finally "gets it." That is, a light suddenly goes on in the student's eye as he or she begins to really understand the material the teacher is imparting.

In fact, a lot of good teachers would tell you that what keeps them going year after year are these magical moments when their instruction hits home with their students, who display genuine understanding and even change their behavior or beliefs based on what they have learned.

This same thing is true to a large degree for preachers. I don't know anyone who enjoys standing before a group of people day after day or week after week without seeing any response. I'm blessed on that score as a pastor, because our church in Dallas is filled with responsive, Spirit-directed people. There is no joy quite like seeing the Spirit of God turn on the light of understanding in people's hearts

as they respond to God's Word. This exciting process is called illumination, and it's a vital part of the doctrine of God's transforming
Word.

The illumination of Scripture follows naturally in the sequence
of God's self-disclosure. Revelation is what God has said about Himself, inspiration is the recording of what God said, and illumination is the process by which God's revelation ceases to be just words
on a page and comes alive in our hearts and minds. Here is a more
formal definition: Illumination is the work of the Holy Spirit that
opens up believers' minds to the Word of God, enabling them to
understand the meaning and personal application of divine revelation. It allows believers to hear God's personal Word to them through
the Scriptures.

THE IMPORTANCE OF ILLUMINATION

The illumination that a student receives in school could be called
natural enlightenment. The difference between this human activity
and supernatural, Holy Spirit–directed enlightenment is crucial for
several reasons. One is that this word is often misused by unbelievers. Some people who have no relationship to Jesus Christ use
terms that sound very similar to biblical terms to describe their
religious experiences, while others turn to the Bible to support all
manner of heresies and offbeat ideas, and then claim that they have
biblical reasons for their views.

Anyone Can Read the Bible

As Christians we need to be precise in our definitions of biblical terms because we aren't the only ones who use them. It seems
that everyone today, from Eastern mystics to New Agers, talks about
being illuminated or enlightened.

But they're on a completely different wavelength, because they
may be using meditation or who knows what other technique or
stimulant to reach their so-called enlightenment. Biblical illumina-

tion must be differentiated from folks who stare at their navels or read tea leaves.

We also need to understand illumination from a biblical standpoint because nonbelievers can read the Bible and claim to understand and follow its message. I'm thinking here of those who try to use the Bible to support heretical teachings. These false teachers very often claim that their views came directly from God in the form of special revelation or illumination.

Now don't misunderstand. A non-Christian who reads the Word with an open heart can come under the Holy Spirit's conviction of the truth and receive Christ. This happens all the time, praise God. But as a rule, when unbelievers read the Bible they do so with a veil over their hearts and minds due to Satan's blinding (see 2 Corinthians 4:3–4; also compare 3:12–16, which speaks of a veil over the minds of Jewish unbelievers). Thus, even if unbelievers understand the Bible academically, there is no connection with its message or author (see John 5:39).

Only the Spirit Can Illumine the Bible

The Spirit's illumination of Scripture may result in a new and deeper understanding of truth we already know, lead us to see truths we never grasped before, cause us to change our beliefs or behavior —or possibly all three. Saul of Tarsus qualified on this score.

Saul was a brilliant young rabbi who knew the Old Testament backward and forward. But it wasn't until Jesus struck Saul down on the Damascus Road (Acts 9) that he really began to understand the Scriptures he had studied all his life, saw new truths about Jesus as the fulfillment of the Mosaic Law, and radically changed his behavior by going from persecutor of Christians to the leading Christian of his day.

We are instructed in the Bible to pray for illumination. A great verse you ought to memorize and pray each day as you open your Bible is this: "Open my eyes, that I may behold wonderful things from Your law" (Psalm 119:18). The psalmist was saying, "Lord, I want to encounter You face-to-face in Your revelation." The entire text of Psalm 119, the longest chapter in the Bible, is an expression of the psalmist's deep love for God's Word and his intense desire to know God.

There are many examples of illumination we could draw on. One dramatic instance is the patriarch Job's encounter with God at the end of his long period of severe testing and suffering. God did a face-to-face with Job in chapters 38–41 that revealed His awesome sovereignty and power and left Job on his face. When it was all over, Job said, "I have heard of You by the hearing of the ear; but now my eyes see You" (42:5). Job was illuminated in a big way—and notice his response in verse 6: "Therefore I retract, and I repent in dust and ashes." Illumination is not always a walk in the park for the one who has been enlightened.

Job's enlightenment is different from ours in at least two important ways. First, God does not confront people today and speak audibly with them the way He did with Job or other people in the Bible such as Moses or Saul. Watch out for people who say God appeared to them or spoke out loud to them. They probably just had too much pizza the night before. God has spoken fully and finally in Jesus (Hebrews 1:1–3), and our responsibility is to respond to His voice in the Word.

A second way that Job's enlightenment differs from ours is that he did not have any written Scriptures that the Spirit of God could point him to and use to enlighten him. Many scholars believe that Job actually predates Moses, the first writer of Scripture. But despite this, Job definitely experienced enlightenment from the Lord.

Job knew and worshiped God before his time of testing, but after God opened Job's eyes in this new way, Job said his previous knowledge was similar to just hearing about someone as opposed to meeting that person face-to-face. I often compare illumination to a blind date. The one making the arrangements can tell you a lot about the person you are going to meet, but it's an entirely different matter to ring the doorbell, or open the door, and see that person for yourself.

THE PROCESS OF ILLUMINATION

The apostle Paul said in 2 Corinthians 3 that in contrast to the veil that covers the Jews' eyes when they read Scripture, believers have "unveiled" faces with which to see the Lord (v. 18). We meet Christ when we come to Him in salvation, but there is another face-to-face meeting with God waiting for us in the pages of His Word. This occurs when we read the Bible and the Spirit turns on the light in our hearts and minds.

God's Light Is Not Automatic

The teaching of illumination reminds us again that nothing is automatic in the Christian life. Have you ever wondered why two Christians can be sitting beside each other in church, hearing the same message with their Bibles open to the same passage, and yet one person is staring blankly into space, not really getting anything, while the other is alive with excitement about what God's Word has to say?

Part of the reason may be the two people's personalities, but there's more to it than that. If the Bible is nothing more than dead words on a page to a Christian, that person may be suffering from a lack of illumination—and it isn't God's fault. We'll talk later about problems that can hinder the Holy Spirit from illuminating God's Word to us.

One way to describe illumination is to say that it's like hearing God call your name. Now hold on, I didn't say you hear God's voice audibly. What I mean is that experience of opening the Word or hearing a sermon and feeling as if that passage was written directly to you. I've had many people say to me over the years, "Pastor, that sermon today had my name on it." When illumination occurs, the Holy Spirit personalizes the Word to you and you see clearly what it is that God wants you to know or do. There is no new revelation from God taking place, but there is new illumination by the Spirit going on every day. If the Spirit were not active in illumination, all of our efforts to understand and personally apply the Bible would be futile.

The Spirit's Work in Illumination

Paul explained why this is so in 1 Corinthians 2:9–16, a classic passage that talks about God's revelation and why we need the Holy Spirit's ministry to understand and apply it. Verses 9–10 make it clear that left on our own, we would never be able to know God: "As it is written, 'Things which eye has not seen and ear has not heard, and which have not entered into the heart of man, all that God has prepared for those who love Him.' For to us God revealed them through the Spirit; for the Spirit searches all things, even the depths of God" (vv. 9–10).

Praise God for the revelation of His Word that opens our spiritual eyes and ears to things that would otherwise be hidden from us. The Holy Spirit was the active agent in communicating the Scripture to its writers, because He is the One who knows "the thoughts of God" (v. 11).

Today the Spirit's primary role in relation to the Bible is illumination, which Paul explained as helping us "know the things freely given to us by God" (v. 12). Only the Spirit can do this, because only the Spirit can teach us "not in words taught by human wisdom, but in those taught by the Spirit, combining spiritual thoughts with spiritual words" (v. 13).

It takes more than human wisdom for illumination to take place. In fact, it usually happens in spite of our "smarts." Jesus thanked His Father that He hid the truth from the "wise and intelligent" who wouldn't humble themselves to receive Christ (Matthew 11:25). Having a string of degrees and a big library will bring you information, but not necessarily illumination. This only comes when the Spirit combines spiritual thoughts, the mind and heart of God, with spiritual words, the revelation of His Word. The Spirit is the true Teacher (see John 14:26; 16:13).

This is how we got our Bible, but it also describes what the Spirit does in our minds and hearts when He turns the light on and we say, "I get it!" I like to illustrate this process by comparing it to the way a photocopy machine reproduces an original document on a piece of blank paper. What the copier does is transfer the original onto the copy so that the copy now "gets it" in terms of receiving the original document. The original in this scenario is the Word of God, and the paper receiving the copy is the believer's heart. The Holy Spirit is the means by which this transfer takes place.

God said that in the new covenant He would institute through the death and resurrection of Jesus, His Word would not be on stone tablets or on scrolls. Instead, "I will put My law within them and on their heart I will write it" (Jeremiah 31:33). So now the Holy Spirit's job is to reproduce the Word, so to speak, so that it shows up on our hearts. And in one sense, when God's Word gets copied onto your heart, you get a huge extra because the Spirit applies the Word to your unique circumstances. This is when the Word becomes God's Word to *you*.

Problems That Can Block the Spirit's Illumination

What can hinder God's work of illumination in a person's life? Sin has produced static on the line between man and God. This is certainly true for unbelievers who are spiritually blind. Paul said that people who are separated from God are "darkened in their understanding" of the truth (Ephesians 4:18). Just as a blind man can't see the sun no matter how much you explain it to him, so the sinner cannot "see" and experience God, because his spiritual receptors are dead.

Paul gave us a classic statement of this fact in 1 Corinthians 2:14: "But a natural man does not accept the things of the Spirit of God, for they are foolishness to him; and he cannot understand them, because they are spiritually appraised."

This is the nonbeliever's condition. But sin can also interrupt a believer's ability to understand and experience God's Word. The writer to the Hebrews delivered a strong rebuke to his readers, who were genuine Christians but were wavering in their commitment: "Concerning him [Melchizedek] we have much to say, and it is hard to explain, since you have become dull of hearing" (Hebrews 5:11).

The writer was in the middle of some deep truth on the priesthood of Melchizedek and how it related to Jesus. But he knew his readers weren't ready to understand it—not because he couldn't explain it, but because the Hebrews had a spiritual reception problem caused by their sin of unbelief as they wavered in their commitment to Christ. They could read the words, but the message wasn't getting through, and thus they were not bringing their lives in line with the truth. Sin blocks our ability to experience God's Word in a life-changing way.

Another problem that can hinder God's work of illumination in a believer's heart is an unwillingness to respond. Someone may say, "Well, it's fine to talk about the need to see beyond the physical. But even though I go to church and read my Bible, I'm not getting any illumination. I'm not getting what other people seem to be getting from the Bible."

I've had people tell me that, and when we talk about it, the real problem usually comes to the surface. The reason many Christians aren't enjoying the Spirit's ministry of illumination is that God knows they aren't going to do anything with the truth. God is not interested in turning on the light of illumination in our hearts just to have us say, "Oh, that's interesting," or "Well, I'm not really ready to do that."

If there is no willingness on our part to apply the Word, God will not illumine the Word to us. Jesus said, "Take care how you listen; for whoever has, to him more shall be given; and whoever does not have, even what he thinks he has shall be taken away from him" (Luke 8:18).

Jesus was talking about our response to God's truth. Believers who respond in obedience to the Word are given more light, while those who hear the Word but don't obey it can actually be worse off for hearing it. One thing that always seems to happen when Christians go off the deep end in some extreme or lapse into doctrinal heresy is that their understanding and/or application of the Word deteriorates. It's as if God withdraws even the illumination they had as they twist or neglect the truth.

Reaching the Highest Possible Level

Illumination is something like reaching the highest level of the three levels of hearing that human beings are capable of. The first level consists of simply receiving the auditory waves that come into our ears. In other words, we hear the sound but it doesn't register in our minds. Parents and married people often get frustrated with their children and spouses when they realize that what they said went in one ear and out the other, as the old saying goes.

We hear on this first level all the time, but we screen out most of the noises or voices around us. This ability is necessary to keep us from being constantly distracted by all the noises of modern-day life—but it's not so helpful when we tune out people we really need to listen to.

I have a friend who works all day, and often into the night, with his radio tuned to a local Christian station. He keeps the volume turned down low, and says he doesn't really "tune in" until he hears a song he likes or a statement from a Bible teacher that pricks his interest. When this happens, he turns up the volume and listens to what is being sung or said.

This process is the second level of hearing, what we could call the understanding level, when we go beyond just picking up sound waves to focusing our minds on what the sounds mean. At this level we can say, like a soldier in the field talking to his commander at headquarters, "Roger, message received." This is obviously an important level of hearing that takes us beyond the first, but there's another level that is much more critical.

This level is reached when the message not only gets into our brains, but down into our bones, so to speak. A parent will often say to his child, "Do you understand what I'm saying to you?" The child may say yes, and even repeat back what was said with great detail and clarity. But until the child responds by obeying the message, he or she hasn't really heard it at all.

God wants to get us to this third level of hearing in which we connect with His Word so completely that we change and arrange our lives in obedience to Him because we see the Word's relevance to our lives. But it takes more than just reading or even studying the Bible to reach this level. It takes the Holy Spirit illuminating the Word in a personal way that reaches us at the core of our being.

The Bible was not written simply as God's autobiography so we can learn important facts about Him. It was written to change us completely inside and out. That's why the best way to study your Bible is not just to open it up and start reading, but to bow your head and ask the Spirit of God to search your heart and cleanse you from any unconfessed sin so that your spiritual eyes and ears can be fully open.

That's the exciting thing about the Spirit's work of illumination. He helps you see what you couldn't see before because you didn't have the right glasses. As I'm writing this book, the conflict in Iraq is still going on. Our soldiers can fight at night because they have special goggles that allow them to see through the darkness.

If you ask God with an honest and open heart to make His Word real to you, you'll find that the words of Scripture will start jumping off the page and into your heart, even when the world around is dark. Then you won't be reading a verse a day to keep the devil away, or because all good Christians are supposed to read the Bible. You'll read God's Word so that He can speak to you personally as His Spirit connects with your human spirit.

THE APPLICATION OF ILLUMINATION

Do you know why so many Christians are discouraged and want to throw in the towel? Because all they see is what they can see with their physical eyes. Look at the secular world around you for a minute. Do you see much out there to make you think God is winning the battle? Probably not, which is why God says we must be able to see beyond the physical realm.

You Have an Anointing from God

Now let me give you a strong word of encouragement concerning the Spirit's work of illumination and the way in which

He connects with believers through the Bible. This is important because many Christians tend to think that this kind of enlightenment is only for people like pastors, teachers, and other spiritual leaders in the body of Christ.

Not so. The apostle John wrote, "You have an anointing from the Holy One, and you all know" (1 John 2:20). All believers are anointed in terms of their ability to receive, understand, and apply truth from the Holy Spirit. In this sense, the anointing is another word for illumination. John went on to say, "The anointing which you received from Him abides in you, and you have no need for anyone to teach you; but as His anointing teaches you about all things, and is true and is not a lie, and just as it has taught you, you abide in Him" (v. 27).

Now it's true that believers differ in their intellectual capacity to deal with and transmit the Word, and some are especially gifted by God in this area. But all believers have an internal "satellite dish," a receiver called the Holy Spirit, to enable them to receive the same signal.

This is the anointing, the divine capacity to receive from God the understanding and personal application of His truth. We can't leave out this step if we want to discover all that God has for us. It's one thing for a woman to hear from the doctor that she is going to be a mother. It's another thing for her to see the sonogram or other image of her developing baby. Just as the sonogram brings light to the "truth" of a baby inside a woman's womb, so the Spirit brings light to God's Word. As we said, it leaps off the page and becomes part of our experience.

Does this mean believers don't need anyone else to help them understand and apply the Word? After all, we just read in 1 John that we don't need anyone to teach us. No, this statement in no way eliminates the need for Bible teachers, who are part of God's gift to the church (see Ephesians 4:11–12). John was writing here about false teachers who were trying to deceive the church (see 1 John 2:18–19), and his point was that believers have the Holy Spirit within to guide them in distinguishing truth from error, and that He can do that even if no human teachers are involved.

If you have ever listened to the spiel of cult members who came knocking on your door, and the Spirit within you said, "This does not agree with My Word," you have experienced what 1 John 2:27 is all about. Because believers have the anointing, John could later write, "Beloved, do not believe every spirit, but test the spirits to see whether they are from God, because many false prophets have gone out into the world" (1 John 4:1).

If you are a believer in Jesus Christ, you have the capacity to distinguish truth from falsehood because the anointing of God is within you to turn on the light and help you see with the eyes of faith what is not visible to your physical sight. It would help a lot if these cultists came around dressed up like demons or something so everyone could see that they are peddling the devil's lies. That way, even when unbelievers who don't know the Bible opened the door, they would scream in fear and slam it shut.

But it doesn't work that way. The Bible says, "Even Satan disguises himself as an angel of light. Therefore it is not surprising if his servants also disguise themselves as servants of righteousness" (2 Corinthians 11:14–15). These cult members are well groomed and all dressed up, and some may even have their children with them to help win a hearing. They carry Bibles and talk about Jesus and heaven—and the unsuspecting and untaught fall for their line every day. It takes keen spiritual sight to see through the deception of false teaching.

This reminds me of the stamp that many theme parks put on your hand either when you come for the day, or when you want to leave for a while and return. The first time my family and I left a theme park during the day, they stamped our hands and we went out. I didn't pay any attention to the stamp, but when we got back to the park later I thought we were in trouble because I didn't see anything on anyone's hands and was afraid the stamps had been rubbed off.

Of course, the stamp was some kind of ink that is invisible to the naked eye, but it becomes visible when they put your hand under a special scanner. I collected a good sermon illustration right there, because it dawned on me that to get access to the "magic kingdom" we wanted to enter, we couldn't use anything from the outside world. Driver's licenses or other photo IDs wouldn't do it. We had to be illuminated by an invisible power source to enjoy the benefits of that kingdom.

You Don't Need a Guru

The anointing also means that Christians don't need to run around all over the place looking for someone to tell them what God wants them to do in applying His Word to their lives.

Now again, I'm not saying that because we are Christians with the Holy Spirit as our illuminator and teacher, we don't need to be under the regular teaching of the Word. After all, you can't live out what you don't understand.

But if you are depending on some spiritual guru or the latest seminar or program to illuminate you and guide you into the specific application He wants you to make with His truth, you are shopping at the wrong mall. God says the anointing is within you in the Person of the Holy Spirit, who according to Jesus "will teach you all things, and bring to your remembrance all that I said to you" (John 14:26). We also learn, "He will guide you into all the truth" (16:13).

Just as the biblical writers were given what God wanted them to write, in a similar way the Holy Spirit gives us what we need to know from the Word to address specific areas in our lives.

Abiding Brings the Anointing

The key to experiencing the illumination of God's Spirit through His Word into your life is "abiding" (1 John 2:24, 27). The abiding of the believer is the assurance we find in the presence and power of Christ when we are living in intimate fellowship with Him and obedience to Him. The anointing flows from abiding.

John used "abide" as his relational term for staying closely and intimately connected to God through His Word. When you abide, you don't just read the Bible as words, but you are looking for the Person behind the words. Abiding says to God, "I want to know and love You more each day and to become more like You." When reading or studying the Bible for knowledge becomes an end in itself rather than the vehicle to cultivate an intimate relationship with God, we miss the power of the anointing.

Look at 1 John 2 again. "The one who says he abides in Him [Christ] ought himself to walk in the same manner as He walked" (v. 6). Again, "The word of God abides in you, and you have overcome the evil one" (v. 14). And then, "As for you, let that abide in you which you heard from the beginning. If what you heard from the beginning abides in you, you also will abide in the Son and in the Father" (v. 24).

Do you see the two-way action here? When we abide in Christ, then His Word abides in us. Does this mean we don't have to do anything but lie around and wait for the Lord to move us? Of course not. One of the paradoxes of the Christian life is that we are to run the race as if everything depended on us, while at the same time trusting and abiding in Christ as if everything depended on Him.

Don't ever get the idea that the Christian life is just "Let go, and let God." God wants to see some motion from us in the form of obedience to His will as expressed in His Word, even before we know what the specifics of His will may be (see John 7:17). Many home alarm systems use motion detectors to intercept intruders. But nothing happens until the alarm senses motion. Too many Christians want to remain where they are without having to move ahead, and yet they want to enjoy the growing blessings and presence of God. But God is saying that when we move, He will make sure that His sensors pick up that movement and give us more of the Spirit's illumination.

The result of illumination is that you get to really experience the spiritual realm firsthand. And unlike my family's trip to the theme park that forced us to take out a small loan, you get your access for free. God wants you to discover "the things freely given to [you] by God" (1 Corinthians 2:12). In other words, the whole kingdom is yours to enjoy. When you are illuminated by the Holy Spirit, the truth of God becomes real to you because it gets down into the deepest levels of your being. That's when the Word becomes so wrapped around your soul, so to speak, that you begin to see and know at a whole new level of seeing and knowing.

The Global Positioning Systems that many cars now have to guide drivers to their destination have both a visual and a verbal element. The system shows you where your car is in relationship to your destination, and a voice gives you specific instructions on how to get there.

The Bible is God's "global positioning system." It gives us the verbal or spoken record of what God has said, and the Holy Spirit illuminates the Word to give us a visual reading, so to speak, as to what we need to do and where we need to go. When these are allowed to do their work in our lives, God through His Word becomes more real to us than we could ever imagine.

9

THE INTERPRETATION OF THE BIBLE

Some years ago I had the privilege of visiting both China and India. Being in each nation was an incredible experience as I got to see entirely different cultures and ways of life in action. But I had several handicaps in these countries because they were foreign territory to me.

My biggest handicap was the inability to speak the language of China or India. I also did not understand all of the people's cultural practices and beliefs, so in some cases I couldn't fully appreciate what I was seeing. I was limited culturally as well as linguistically, and I needed someone to help me maneuver my way through these lands that were new and strange to me.

When they meet someone who is obviously a visitor, Texans say, "You aren't from these parts, are you?" I most definitely was not from any "parts" of China or India, and my trips might have been disasters except for one factor: I had an interpreter to stand beside me and translate what I was hearing into a language I could understand and respond to.

If you have ever tried to communicate with someone in another language, you know how difficult that can be. Even with an interpreter who knows both languages, there are always times when you are stymied either because the interpreter is groping for the right word in the other language to accurately convey your English word, or vice versa. And interpretation is almost never just a matter of doing a straight word-for-word translation.

In fact, this is often impossible. I'm told that the Spanish equivalent of the expression "to burn the midnight oil" means literally "to singe the eyebrows." Even when a word-for-word translation is attempted, it sometimes yields a meaning so far off the mark as to be comical.

I heard about an example of this in which Matthew 26:41, "The spirit is willing, but the flesh is weak," was fed into a Russian-language translation machine. The sentence that came out said, "The whiskey is agreeable, but the meat has gone bad."

Now you may think this only happens when going from one language to another. But some folk who speak the same language and even live under the same roof still can't communicate with each other. Language can be a huge barrier to communication when there is uncertainty about the meaning of our words.

I can illustrate this by mentioning the word *lead*. Now you have no way of knowing for sure which meaning I have in mind until I give it some context by using it in a sentence. That's because these four simple letters can be a verb that means "to direct," a noun that means "a position in front," or an adjective that means "to act or serve as the lead," as in the lead story in a newspaper.

These meanings are at least related in concept, but they don't exhaust the possibilities for confusion. The word *lead* has an entirely different meaning, and even a different pronunciation, when it refers to a soft metal. And even beyond this we have the word *led* that sounds just like the soft metal, but is the past tense of the verb *lead*.

So now even if I was talking to you and told you I was thinking of the word *lead,* and pronounced it with the short *e* instead of the long *e,* you still couldn't be absolutely certain what I meant until I used my word in a sentence that clarified its meaning.

In other words, you are in the dark until I interpret the word I am using and thus reveal its meaning to you so we can understand each other. Now if one small and seemingly simple word like *lead* requires that much interpretation to make sense, think of all the possibilities for miscommunication and misunderstanding in the hundreds of thousands of words in the English language—to say nothing of the thousands of other languages and dialects on earth. According to one linguistic expert, the five hundred most often used English words have an average of twenty-three meanings each. It's no wonder that communication demands understanding to be effective, even between people who are speaking the same language.

Now let's take this one step further and think about how totally ill-equipped sinful human beings are to understand God's message from heaven without someone to interpret it to us. If you think you have problems trying to understand your teenager or your spouse, you haven't seen anything yet. How could a perfectly holy God communicate with a sinful race on a tiny speck of His creation called Earth? He did it in two ways: by becoming a man Himself in the Person of His Son, and by giving us His written Word in human languages that were designed to be read and understood.

THE HOLY SPIRIT IS
THE BIBLE'S DIVINE INTERPRETER

You may remember from your high school or college classes that communication involves three elements. There is an encoder, the person sending the message; a decoder, the person receiving the message; and the message itself. The goal of communication is to make sure that the data the decoder receives is what the encoder intended to send so the message doesn't get lost in transit.

The Holy Spirit Gave Us the Bible

We don't have to worry that the message got distorted during the transmission of the Bible from God's mouth to our hands. God Himself is the encoder in the Person of the Holy Spirit, and the message is His Word sent to the "decoders," the human writers of Scripture.

These men would have been the fallible link in this infallible chain, but the Spirit took care of that by moving them to write under His inspiration in order to deliver the exact message God wanted to communicate. From Moses, who wrote the first five books of the Bible around 1400 B.C., to the apostle John, who wrote Revelation in about A.D. 90, the Holy Spirit made sure there was no accuracy lost in the transmission of Scripture. Without this, it would have been impossible for the message to stay on track over such a huge gap of time with so many different people involved.

We Need to Know What the Bible Is Saying

I said in the previous chapter that our task is not to receive new revelation, but to understand the revelation God has given us. This task is interpretation, or the work of determining what the Holy Spirit meant by what He inspired the Bible's authors to record. Many people avoid the Bible because they say they can't understand it. The Bible is often a closed book to people, even though there are dozens of translations available in clear and readable English.

When people say they can't understand the Bible, they are usually talking about the issue of interpretation. The technical word for this is *hermeneutics,* a word that comes straight from the Greek and is related to the god Hermes of Greek mythology, whose job was to communicate the language of the gods to human beings. Hermeneutics is the science and art of interpreting the Bible.

Interpretation is a science because words have meanings that we can rely on, and languages follow certain rules of grammar and composition that can be observed and cataloged. But interpretation is also an art because, as we learned from the example of the Russian "translation" of Matthew 26:41, just trying to match up words from one language to another is not enough to decipher what an author is saying.

The Holy Spirit Knows What the Word Means

There is a great example of our need for interpretation in the evangelist Philip's encounter with the Ethiopian eunuch, as recorded in Acts 8:26–40. You can read the entire story, which only takes a minute and may be familiar to you. This Ethiopian was an official of the royal court who had come to Jerusalem to worship the true God and was returning home, sitting in his chariot and reading from the book of Isaiah (v. 28).

The Holy Spirit told Philip to go meet this man, and, when Philip did, he heard him reading aloud from Isaiah 53. Now let's stop here for a minute, because Isaiah 53 is a passage that begs for interpretation. We understand it to be speaking of Christ, because the suffering described there matches what happened in His crucifixion to such an amazing degree that this can be nothing else but a prophecy of Jesus' death. Besides, this one is easy because this is the interpretation that Philip gave to the eunuch (v. 35), which means we have the Bible interpreting itself. And when it comes to understanding Scripture, it doesn't get any better than that.

But leaving Acts 8 aside for now, notice that in Isaiah's writings God does not identify this sufferer as the Messiah, or as Jesus, but as "My servant" (Isaiah 52:13). Some Jews believe this is speaking of the Messiah who is yet to come, but others say that the servant is the nation of Israel itself. So it's understandable that the eunuch was puzzled about the identity of this person when Philip asked him the classic interpretive question: "Do you understand what you are reading?" (v. 30).

The eunuch didn't know about the Holy Spirit's role as the Inspirer and Interpreter of Scripture, so he answered, "Well, how could I, unless someone guides me?" (v. 31). So Philip became his interpreter that day under the Spirit's guidance as he "preached Jesus to him" (v. 35).

So here we have a man who was reading the Bible, but not understanding it because no interpretation was taking place. He could read the words on the scroll, and he certainly understood what it meant, for instance, for a sheep to be slaughtered. The problem for him was that Isaiah 53 did not identify the one who was to die, and the eunuch was eager to know who it was.

We Need an Interpreter to Understand the Bible

How many times have you read your Bible while wondering what the writer was talking about? We need the ministry of interpretation because it is possible to read something without grasping it. When you read your Bible but don't understand it, then your ability to apply the Scripture properly to your life is hindered.

Now it's important to understand something before we go any further. When we talk about the meaning of a Bible text, we are after the original author's intent and not just what it says to us. Many Christians think that doing Bible study consists of going around the room while people tell one by one what the verse or passage in question means to them.

But that's not interpreting the Bible, because one of the principles of good biblical interpretation is that a text has one primary meaning. It may have many personal applications, but the Bible does not mean whatever anyone wants it to mean. Most heresies begin with a twisted interpretation of the Scripture. Building a spiritually healthy faith has to begin with the correct interpretation of God's Word.

Some husbands and wives need an interpreter to help them build a healthy marriage, because even though words are passing between them in the same language, the meaning is getting completely lost. When two people are talking but not really communicating, the conflict often gets worse the longer they talk. In these situations one person will usually get upset and walk away, saying, "Oh, forget it." It's frustrating when there is no understanding of what is being said.

Sometimes poor interpretation can have bigger consequences than just frustration. As a boy I suffered horrifically with asthma, and every week I had to go to the hospital to get shots. On top of that I wanted to try all the sports, so I was constantly battling this illness.

Once, when I was about thirteen years old, I went to the doctor, and he prescribed the wrong medicine. I took it and almost died that night. I'll never forget the sight of my father, standing over the bed with tears in his eyes watching me gasp for breath and going into convulsions because a doctor misinterpreted my condition and applied the wrong medication.

I use this example to remind us that the goal of accurately interpreting the Bible is not just understanding for its own sake, but understanding so as to apply the Word correctly to our lives. Our church in Dallas has a ministry to people who are hearing impaired so they can join fully in the ministry of the Word. We do this because our goal is not to fill the pews, but to help every believer understand and obey God's Word. The exciting thing is that when you arrive at the right understanding of the Bible along with the right application, there is no issue in life that cannot be addressed victoriously. Understanding and application join together to bring about transformation.

THERE ARE PREREQUISITES
TO INTERPRETING SCRIPTURE

The Bible is meant to be an open book to anyone who wants to know the truth. But this does not mean that God simply throws His treasure chest of truth open to anyone who comes along so the person can look it over and take whatever he wants. Jesus called that "throw[ing] your pearls before swine" (Matthew 7:6). This means to give something valuable to folks who don't value it and therefore treat it with contempt. Certain prerequisites must be present in our lives before the Bible becomes an open book to us.

We Must Know Christ as Our Savior

The Bible teaches that every believer is a priest before God. Peter called the church "a royal priesthood" (1 Peter 2:9). A priest's job was to stand between the people and God and intercede for them, while also bringing back God's message and will to them. But the office of priest is no longer needed now that Christ's death has opened the way into God's presence for every believer.

The doctrine of the priesthood of the believer means that we do not need someone else to hear from God for us and tell us what He said. All Christians have the anointing and don't need a teacher in the sense of someone to represent them before God while they stand by and wait to see what God says (see 1 John 2:27). God gives us pastors and teachers to guide us, but all true believers are qualified to hear from God by virtue of their salvation and the gift of the indwelling Holy Spirit.

So the first qualification to understand the Bible is to be saved. Paul said "a natural man," or unsaved person, considers the things of God to be "foolishness" because they are "spiritually appraised" (1 Corinthians 2:14). A nonbeliever does not have the capacity to interpret divine truth.

We Must Be in Fellowship with the Holy Spirit

A second prerequisite is intimate communion with God through the Holy Spirit. The closer you are to the Spirit, the more clearly you will understand the Word. This follows because the Holy Spirit is "the Spirit of truth" (John 16:13) whom God sent to continue the teaching Jesus began while He was on earth. One of Jesus' titles was Teacher (see Mark 4:38 and John 11:28), a ministry that was handed over to the Spirit when Jesus went back to heaven. If you want to learn a teacher's material, you can't do any better than to hang out with the teacher.

The Holy Spirit's job is to interpret and clarify the truth—to reveal to you what it means and how you need to apply it to your life. But the Spirit does not do His work of teaching in a heart and mind that are closed to Him. I am referring to a believer who is out of sync with the Spirit for whatever reason. Since the Holy Spirit is the Illuminator and the Interpreter of Scripture, it makes sense that the closer you are to Him, the more the Bible will become clear to you, while the farther you are from the Spirit, the more God's Word will become fuzzy and out of focus (see John 16:13).

Sometimes the Spirit works directly with a Christian who is reading the Word when the light suddenly comes on. Perhaps you have read a passage of Scripture that you have read many times before, but this time the words jump off the page and you understand the passage in a way you never had before.

This is the Holy Spirit's work, and He can do it with or without study aids or human teachers. The Spirit may have brought to mind another part of Scripture that helped explain the text you were reading, or used a devotional book or some other help to unlock the Scripture. He also uses the ministry of pastors and teachers to communicate His truth. I would not step into the pulpit if I did not believe that the Holy Spirit could take my hours of Bible study as I put them into words in a sermon, and use those words to help open up His Word to people's understanding.

Philip was being guided by the Spirit as he explained the Scriptures to the Ethiopian eunuch in Acts 8. The Bible also says that when Peter had finished his sermon on the Day of Pentecost, the people "were pierced to the heart" (Acts 2:37) and cried out for help in knowing what to do next. The Holy Spirit is behind the human teachers whose job it is to help God's people understand His Word.

We Must Be Willing to Grow as We Learn

A third prerequisite to understanding the Bible has to do with our willingness to respond in obedience to what the Spirit shows us (see Psalm 119:34). Peter wrote, "Therefore, putting aside all malice and all deceit and hypocrisy and envy and all slander, like newborn babies, long for the pure milk of the word, so that by it you may grow in respect to salvation" (1 Peter 2:1–2). God wants us to get rid of any sinful attitude that prevents us from growing as we feed on His Word.

If a baby is being fed properly and yet is not growing, he needs to see a doctor, because a baby's body is designed to grow when given the right nourishment. The same is true of believers, and if growth is not happening, then we need to find out what is wrong and deal with it. We can be sure the problem is not with the Word. It is "pure milk," filled with all the right nutrients and free of impurities.

Normally a child who isn't growing properly physically did not choose that condition and can't do anything about it. But when it comes to the Bible, we have a choice whether to be healthy or stunted in our growth. We must cooperate with the Holy Spirit who desires to teach us. That's why I said there must be a willingness on our part to grow.

One aspect of this involves a crucial spiritual principle we encountered earlier. This is what we could call the "obey before you know" principle; that is, we must be committed to obey God even before He reveals the specifics of His will and Word to us. You may take a car out for a test-drive to see if you like the way it handles and feels before you commit yourself to buy it, but you don't take God's truth out for a test-drive to see if it's something you want to do.

An unwillingness to obey God helps to explain why some Christians can go to church for decades, and yet their understanding is muted and their growth is stunted. God's Word is transforming, but they aren't transformed by it because they are not willing to submit to God. Some of these people may know the Bible in terms of being able to quote it or find the stories. But knowledge is not equivalent to obedience. In fact, Paul said that without spiritual transformation, "Knowledge makes arrogant" (1 Corinthians 8:1).

INTERPRETING THE BIBLE
INVOLVES SPECIFIC STEPS

Having said that knowledge of the Bible alone is not enough, let me add that knowledge of the Word is the right place to start. Learning the Bible takes work. That's why Paul told Timothy, "Be diligent to present yourself approved to God as a workman who does not need to be ashamed, accurately handling the word of truth" (2 Timothy 2:15).

The First Step Is to Read the Bible

Now this may sound intimidating, and some people are called to devote their lives to the study and teaching of Scripture. But the fact is that a lot of Christians don't advance in their knowledge and understanding of Scripture because they simply don't take the first and seemingly obvious step, which is to read the Bible with consistency and concentration.

These are the folks who read a verse a day to keep the devil away, or who turn to the Bible during a crisis for a word of hope or direction. It's OK to ask God to give you a word from the Word when you are in a crisis. But make no mistake. This kind of approach to the Bible is the exception, not the pattern. But a lot of people just want a little bit of Bible here and there to get them through the tough spots because they don't want to be consistent workmen.

If you have never gotten lost in the wonder of the Word as you read and meditated on it, you are missing one of the great delights of the Christian life. There is tremendous power in simply reading the Bible, because there is more at work than just your mind and ability to remember. The Holy Spirit is weaving those truths together as you read, until one day you discover that two and two is adding up to four and God's Word is making sense to you. Reading the Bible is the first step to interpreting it.

The Second Step Is to Ask Some Questions

Another step is to ask some very basic interpretive questions about the passage you are reading. For instance, what does the text say? That is, try paraphrasing it back to yourself or summarizing what the passage says.

Then you might ask to whom this passage was written, and under what circumstances. Knowing a passage's original recipients and context can help unlock its meaning. Many Christians can quote Philippians 4:19, the promise that God will meet all of our needs according to His riches in Christ. But this is part of a larger context in which Paul thanked the Philippians for their faithful and sacrificial giving in support of his ministry (vv. 14–18). So the promise of God's supply is tied to our faithfulness in giving to His work.

It's amazing how many times people overlook the context or the recipients of a Bible text. Many of the twisted Bible teachings floating around today could be untwisted really fast if these basic principles of interpretation were applied. Cults love to rip individual Bible verses out of their context.

Other basic interpretive questions to ask of any Bible passage include these: Is there a command here to be obeyed, a sin to avoid, a promise to claim, or a warning to heed? These are just some of the questions you can use to understand the Word. You should also have some basic Bible study tools such as a concordance that lists every word in the Bible, a good Bible commentary, and a Bible dictionary. There are available several excellent one- or two-volume commentaries on the whole Bible.

Every effort we make to correctly understand the Bible is part of what Paul called "accurately handling the word of truth." This means to make a straight cut, which is interesting because as a tentmaker Paul no doubt had to be careful and accurate as he cut animal skins or other material to make his tents. The idea is to cut on the dotted line and not veer off. The Bible has specific and definite meanings that can be determined by careful, hard, Holy Spirit–directed work.

The Most Important Step Is to Look for Jesus

I have saved the most important interpretive key for last because it deserves special treatment. The key to understanding the Bible is to see how it relates to Jesus Christ. Christ is *the* key to the Scriptures (see John 5:39).

The Old Testament points to Jesus Christ. John the Baptist made that clear when he said of Jesus, "Behold, the Lamb of God who takes away the sin of the world!" (John 1:29). What John was saying is that the entire sacrificial system of the Mosaic Law pointed forward to Jesus. Today, the entire New Testament points backward to Jesus. He is the living incarnate Word of God, and He and the living written Word always agree. Find Jesus in your passage, and you will be on the right track to its meaning.

Something very exciting happens when you begin to rightly interpret the truth of God's Word and see its connection to Jesus. Just ask the two disciples who were on their way home to Emmaus from Jerusalem on the day of Jesus' resurrection (Luke 24:13–32). They were depressed because they didn't really believe Jesus had risen, so He showed up to give them an unforgettable Bible lesson.

When Jesus came alongside these two men and asked them what was happening, they told Him all about their hopes that this Man called Jesus was the Messiah. They also poured out their deep disappointment that apparently He was not the one because He had been killed and buried.

Now here is where I want to zero in on the story. Jesus let these two disciples know that their problem was not that He had let them down. Their real problem was a faulty and very limited understanding of Scripture. Jesus hit the problem on the head when He said, "O foolish men and slow of heart to believe in all that the prophets have spoken! Was it not necessary for the Christ to suffer these things and to enter into His glory?" (vv. 25–26).

Now notice what happened next. "Then beginning with Moses and with all the prophets, He explained to them the things concerning Himself in all the Scriptures" (v. 27). Jesus opened the Old

Testament to page one, so to speak, and showed these men how all the Scriptures spoke of Him and pointed toward His death and resurrection. By this time they had arrived home in Emmaus, and wanted Jesus to stay. But He disappeared from their sight, and they said to each other, "Were not our heats burning within us while He was speaking to us on the road, while he was explaining the Scriptures to us?" (v. 32).

When God opens the truth of His Word to your understanding, your heart will burn with new excitement and new insight. The Word can burn away your sense of hopelessness, your fear, your depression because it seems like nothing is going to work out right. A heart on fire with the Word of God will lift your head from despair. The Bible calls God "the One who lifts my head" (Psalm 3:3). In Nehemiah 8, when the people of God heard His Word as it was read to them, they threw a party because they were full of joy at understanding the Scriptures.

God the Holy Spirit wants to guide you into "all the truth" (John 16:13). He doesn't just want you to be under the teaching of the Word, but to also be *in* the Word. He wants to make His Word burn in your heart, because when that happens and you apply what the Holy Spirit of God is teaching you, you will be changed by the power of His transforming Word.

10

THE CANONICITY OF THE BIBLE

There is an old story about a mountain man who finally decided to let his boy go down to the school in the "flatlands" for some "book learnin'."

One day the man visited the school carrying his squirrel rifle on his shoulder and met the teacher, who was glad he had come and wanted to impress him. "Oh," she said, displaying the textbooks, "this semester we will be studying English, history, science, and math. In fact, we are going to study trigonometry."

The man scratched his head for a minute, and then his face brightened. "Say, make sure my boy gets plenty of that there 'triggernometry.' He's the worst shot in the family!"

That mountain man isn't the only person who ever got confused about the contents of a subject. I can imagine that when some people hear the words *canon* or *canonicity* of Scripture, they must think, *Wow! I knew the Bible had power, but I didn't realize it had firepower!* Canonicity is a subject you don't hear much about, but as you can tell by the spelling of the word, it has nothing to do with weapons. The canonicity of Scripture is a very important part of bibliology, the doctrine or study of the Bible.

The word *canon* is from the ancient world and basically means a rule or standard. It referred to a reed that was used to measure things, much as we would use a ruler today. The classic definition of canon in church life is "rule of faith." Over the centuries of church history, many denominations and church bodies have drawn up canons that help to determine belief and practice for their people. The Roman Catholic Church has an extensive body of canon law that has been collected and revised over many centuries—and the Roman church also has its own canon of Scripture. Later we're going to see how it differs from the Protestant canon.

In the process of time the word *canon* also came to mean a catalog or list—in this case, the authoritative list of books that make up the Bible. Canonization tells how the Bible received its acceptance as men recognized the authority of God's inspired writings. It is the process by which God's inspired word was recognized by men of God and then collected and preserved by the people of God. This subject is as intriguing as it is important, because the process by which the books of the Bible were included is an amazing story in itself and one that's filled with drama. But my primary concern is the product that we have in our hands today, the thirty-nine Old Testament books and twenty-seven New Testament books that make up God's inspired, inerrant Word.

The fact that so many Christians have never been introduced to the subject of canonicity means that some of the material in this chapter may be news to some readers. For instance, it may be news to you that there exist several different lists of books that are considered to be part of the Bible. You may also not be aware that there were many other so-called gospels, epistles, and other manuscripts written around the same time as the Bible that did not make it into the Scriptures. And it may surprise you to know that some church leaders questioned the authenticity of several New Testament epistles.

These things are part of the drama of canonicity, but here's the bottom line: The same God who spoke His Word, inspired holy men to record every word exactly as He wanted it, and then preserved His Word through every attempt to destroy or deny it, also oversaw the process by which the sixty-six books of the Bible were assembled into the complete and authoritative collection of Scripture.

THE BOOKS OF THE BIBLE WERE DISCERNED

The first question that needs to be answered concerning the Bible's canonicity is how some writings were chosen to be included in the Scripture, while others were excluded. The key is in the title I've given to this section. What the early church did was discern, under the guidance of the Holy Spirit, which books *already* carried the stamp of the Spirit's inspiration, and which did not. In other words, a body of church leaders did not sit down and read, say, the Gospel of Matthew, and then take a vote as to whether they thought it was inspired or not, with the majority vote winning.

The Bible's Books Have Their Own Authority

Now that may sound confusing at first, because in fact the church *did* have to draw the line and either include or exclude particular books. But there is all the difference in the world between discerning what is already true, and deciding whether it's true or not by human judgment and majority vote. The determining authority for the canon of Scripture was God Himself, not any church body or individual leader. God decided the canon of Scripture; men simply recognized it.

Let me give you an everyday example of what we're talking about. Suppose you sell something during your Saturday garage sale for one hundred dollars. On Monday, you go down to your bank to deposit the five crisp, new twenty-dollar bills the buyer gave you on Saturday—but the bank teller informs you to your horror that her electronic scanner shows all of the bills to be counterfeit.

Now after you recover your breath, you can protest all you want, and remind her that you accepted the bills in good faith. You can say that the buyer seemed as honest as Abe Lincoln, and even claimed to be a close friend and associate of the bank's president. You can show the teller that the phony bills all have Andrew Jackson's picture on them, just like the other twenty-dollar bills in her till. You can even gather all the customers in the bank around and take a vote on whether the bills look and feel authentic to them.

But none of that matters, because you are still going to be out a hundred bucks—and you'll probably have the FBI calling you for an interview. The fact is that the standard for authentic U.S. bills has already been determined, and yours don't cut it.

Now transfer this scenario to the Bible. Let's consider Matthew, which was written by one of Jesus' twelve apostles. There was also a text floating around in the early church that claimed to be a "gospel" written by the apostle Thomas, who was just as authentic an apostle as Matthew. And the Gospel of Thomas was just one of dozens of so-called gospels and epistles in existence that claimed divine authority. How did the early church know that the gospel of Matthew was part of God's authentic revelation, while the gospel of Thomas was a fraud? And how can we be sure today that we're not missing something God wanted us to know, but that got left out of the Bible?

The answer is that the church ran both books under the "scanner" of the Holy Spirit's sovereign guidance and direction, and the Gospel of Thomas didn't cut it. Church leaders examined the books carefully for internal evidence of inspiration, and checked out the external evidence for their authenticity, following specific criteria by which a book claiming to be Scripture either authenticated or disqualified itself.

We must understand this fundamental principle that God the Holy Spirit, and not man, determined the canon of Scripture. If we do not believe and affirm that the God who guided human beings to write Scripture also guided other human beings to collect it into one book, then our entire doctrine of Scripture crumbles like a house of cards.

Let me say it again. The church only recognized the canon that God established. That's a very important distinction, because if man determines what is Scripture, then man can add to it or take away from it.

Canonicity Is a Critical Issue Today

Someone might say, "Tony, is this really a big deal? I mean, come on. The Bible has been the way it is for hundreds and hundreds of years. This is not something we need to get worked up about, is it?"

Absolutely. Canonicity is not just a musty issue from ancient history. American founding father Thomas Jefferson, who was a deist, took a pair of scissors to the Gospels and cut out the parts he didn't accept. But we have a much more recent example than that.

As I'm writing this book, a mega-best-selling novel entitled *The DaVinci Code* is claiming that there was an entire period of Jesus' life that was written down but was suppressed by the church because it conflicted with the "official" story of Jesus as recorded in Scripture. The issue of the Bible's canonicity is being hotly debated on all the networks and talk shows at this very moment, although you will probably not hear the word *canon* used very often.

The canon is something like gravity. You and I didn't create the law of gravity, and we can't control it. All we can do is recognize, use, and submit to this law that God created. You don't have to like the law of gravity for it to be in effect. You may even announce that you are taking an "anti-canonical" view toward gravity and no longer consider yourself subject to it, but are open to the possibility that a later discovery will amend or invalidate it.

But gravity is a law, or a canon, of God's world that says what goes up, must come down. This is the standard that has been established, and your decision to demonstrate your freedom from gravity by jumping out of a tenth-floor window won't change anything except the way your body is arranged. So it is with those who have tried to ignore, defy, and deny the truth that God superintended the process by which each of the sixty-six inspired books was admitted into the Bible's canon.

THE BIBLE HAD "ADMISSION STANDARDS"

Every college or university has certain standards that applicants must meet before being admitted. Schools differ in the details of their admission standards, but they usually include such basics as a high school diploma, a certain minimum score on standard achievement or admissions tests, evidence of financial ability to pay for school, a medical exam to determine the applicant's health, along with personal references and/or recommendations from recognized authorities who can vouch for the fact that this person can handle the work and is worthy of being admitted to the school.

There were also admission standards that had to be met for a piece of writing to be recognized as Spirit-inspired and admitted to the canon of the New Testament. There were several very critical tests the early church used during this process. The two basic criteria were that a book had to carry the authority of an apostle, and had to be recognized and accepted by the church. Within these standards there are various subpoints, which we will discuss as we go.

A Book Had to Have the Right Authority

For a book to be admitted into the Bible, it had to have been written by a true prophet or apostle, or by someone in direct contact with them. The legitimacy and authenticity of this message was confirmed by accompanying supernatural acts of God (Acts 2:22; 2 Corinthians 12:12; Hebrews 2:4). Thus Matthew, and John's and Peter's writings, met that standard. Books like Mark, Luke, Acts, James, and Jude qualified because they were written by firsthand associates of the twelve apostles, men who carried the apostles' stamp of approval. Paul's epistles bore the stamp of apostolic authorship because God called him to be the apostle to the Gentiles. Hebrews is the only New Testament book whose author we don't know for sure.

Just as a contender for the New Testament had to meet the standard of apostolic authority, the standards were extremely high for inclusion in the Old Testament canon. The writer of Hebrews affirmed that God "spoke long ago to the fathers in the prophets in many portions and in many ways" (1:1).

The first prophet that God spoke through was Moses. We get a glimpse of this in Exodus 24:3–4: "Then Moses came and recounted to the people all the words of the Lord and all the ordinances; and all the people answered with one voice and said, 'All the words which the Lord has spoken we will do!' Moses wrote down all the words of the Lord."

God spoke His revelation and Moses wrote it down by inspiration. Moses made a written record of what God told him. The reason we know that God created the heavens and the earth is that God the Holy Spirit inspired Moses to record these events, even though no human being was present at creation. Moses did not just sit down, look up at the stars, and begin weaving stories about God.

In fact, God established very strict guidelines for His prophets that help us draw the line between true and false prophets even today. God said to Moses:

> I will raise up a prophet from among their countrymen like you, and I will put My words in his mouth, and he shall speak to them all that I command him. It shall come about that whoever will not listen to My words which he shall speak in My name, I Myself will require it of him. But the prophet who speaks a word presumptuously in My name which I have not commanded him to speak, or which he speaks in the name of other gods, that prophet shall die. (Deuteronomy 18:18–20)

You can see why there wasn't a long line of people volunteering to be prophets in Old Testament days. If you tried to claim a true prophet's authority falsely, it would cost you your life. A prophet had an awesome responsibility because he had to speak the very words of God, just as he received them from God, and the words he received from God became the standard by which God's people would be judged. Thus, for a book to be recognized as canonical it had to tell the truth from God and had to be true about God (Deuteronomy 13:1–3).

By the time Moses was dead and Joshua had succeeded him as God's leader for Israel, Joshua had the writings of Moses to read and obey. That's why God commanded Joshua, "This book of the law shall not depart from your mouth, but you shall meditate on it day and night, so that you may be careful to do according to all that is written in it; for then you will make your way prosperous, and then you will have success" (Joshua 1:8).

But then Joshua wrote the book that bears his name and added to the writings of Scripture. Joshua passed the test of being associated with a prophet with flying colors. He was Moses' right-hand man. In the last chapter of Joshua we are told: "And Joshua wrote these words in the book of the law of God; and he took a large stone and set it up there under the oak that was by the sanctuary of the Lord" (24:26). Joshua had the writings of Moses, but he also wrote under the Spirit's inspiration. This is how the Bible accumulated over time as there developed a recognized chain of prophetic leaders whose writings were accepted as Scripture (2 Chronicles 9:29). These men knew they were hearing from God (Jeremiah 1:2; Ezekiel 3:1).

When it comes to the Old Testament canon, we have a witness to the authenticity of the books that goes back even before the beginning of the church. The Jews had recognized and brought together the books of the Hebrew canon many years before the days of Jesus and the apostles. In other words, God led the Jews to assemble their inspired canon—and the fact that God's people rejected a batch of other Jewish books, called the Apocrypha, is critically important, as we will see in a minute.

Each of the New Testament books except Hebrews carries the name either of an apostle or a personal associate of an apostle. And the apostles, particularly Paul, were not reluctant to claim God's inspiration for their writings.

For instance, Paul wrote, "For I would have you know, brethren, that the gospel which was preached by me is not according to man. For I neither received it from man, nor was I taught it, but I received it through a revelation of Jesus Christ" (Galatians 1:11–12). And again, "For this reason we also constantly thank God that when you received the word of God which you heard from us, you accepted it not as the word of men, but for what it really is, the word of God, which also performs its work in you who believe" (1 Thessalonians 2:13).

If you'll allow me a word of application at this point, this verse has something very crucial to say about the way we hear and receive the Scriptures today. I know I am not the only pastor who preaches the Word as clearly and faithfully as possible, and yet often wonders why it doesn't seem to "work." The answer in many cases lies in the fact that Christians too often receive the Word as the word of man, not of God. They say, "Oh, that's just what the preacher says. I don't have to buy it." If you believe that the Bible is just the word of one human being to another, it won't carry the authority that God wants it to have in your life. You may even like the sermon you heard last Sunday and agree with every word of it, but the Word is not having the authority it is meant to have until you put it to work on Monday. As a pastor, I pray every week that God will remove whatever is of me in the message so that His Word can be heard and believed in all of its power.

The apostles knew their writings were authoritative, and said so. But even Luke, who was not an apostle, was bold to say that he received the material for both volumes of his writings from the apostles (see Luke 1:1–4 and Acts 1:2). And in a very important passage, Paul's writings received the apostolic seal of approval from Peter, who called Paul's letters "the Scriptures" (2 Peter 3:15–16).

A Book Had to Be Accepted by the People of God

Another test of canonicity was whether the people of God recognized it as authoritative and accepted it as the Word of God. In other words, a book had to win a hearing from God's people as the Holy Spirit witnessed within them that the book's message was from God (see Nehemiah 8:9, 14–18; 1 Thessalonians 2:13).

We have seen that the Hebrew canon was already established by the time of Jesus. Our Lord quoted extensively from the Old

Testament during His earthly ministry, and in so doing validated the writings of the patriarchs and prophets (Matthew 26:56; Luke 24:27). The appearance of Moses and Elijah with Jesus on the Mount of Transfiguration (see Matthew 17:3) was a powerful testimony of their authority as representatives of these two categories of Old Testament authors, and also a powerful testimony that all of the Old Testament points to Jesus.

Notice how Paul also testified to the authority of the Old Testament, and urged the church to make use of it in learning how God wants us to live. Paul wrote, "For whatever was written in earlier times [the Old Testament] was written for our instruction, so that through perseverance and the encouragement of the Scriptures we might have hope" (Romans 15:4). Elsewhere Paul said the events in the Old Testament "happened to them as an example, and they were written for our instruction" (1 Corinthians 10:11). The New Testament quotes the Old Testament more than 250 times, and alludes to it another 900 times. This is overwhelming evidence that the apostles considered the Old Testament to be God's authoritative Word.

The Gospels came to the church bearing the stamp of inspiration. The New Testament epistles were used in the church and circulated among the churches, and they gained instant recognition as the Word of God. The teachings of the apostles were considered authoritative for the church (see 1 Corinthians 14:37; 1 Thessalonians 2:4). The authors of these books often claimed inspiration for themselves (see Galatians 1:11–12; 1 Thessalonians 2:13). And the apostles' doctrines are consistent with one another—another key test of canonicity.

So what happened to the dozens and dozens of false books like the Gospel of Thomas that people tried to put forward as Scripture? The church examined and rejected them, either finding that their claim to be of apostolic authorship was false, or that their teachings were foolish at best and heretical at worst. Some books failed on both of these counts. But the true works of Scripture gained a wide acceptance because the church recognized their inspiration.

SOME CLOSING OBSERVATIONS
ON THE CANON OF SCRIPTURE

I want to make some other observations that are important to this study. The canon of Scripture was compiled over time, not being fully settled until about four hundred years after Christ. And even then some books continued to be questioned by various leaders and councils, including 2 Peter, 2 and 3 John, James, Jude, Hebrews, and even Revelation.

The Doubted Books in Scripture

Now some people point to these things as evidence that the process of assembling the canon was a subjective human work. Actually, they prove just the opposite. The fact that the canon of Scripture existed by informal recognition for so long shows the staying power of the books that God inspired. For instance, the Gospel of Thomas had basically several hundred years to convince the church that it was real, yet it did not make it into the canon because it is not Scripture. The lateness of the final canon is testimony to the fact that what the church had recognized and accepted all along as Scripture was valid.

Some Christians get uncomfortable when they learn that some of the New Testament books were questioned for many years. If you feel that way, you have nothing to worry about. Again, the fact that each of the books named above survived its doubters and was either accepted into, or allowed to remain in, the canon is very significant.

Most of the doubts had to do with the apostolic authorship of these books, but they proved their inspiration. Many of the doubts about James stemmed from a misunderstanding of James's teaching that we are saved by works and not by faith alone. Careful study and exposition of James has shown that those who thought James contradicted Paul's ringing declaration, "The righteous man shall live by faith" (Romans 1:17), were simply wrong. James complements Paul by telling us that we are justified in the eyes of others by our works.

The book of Revelation was the last book of Scripture to be written, and the end of the canon. It was questioned in part because its apocalyptic images seemed too fantastic to be real, but again that doubt was settled by careful biblical interpretation.

John claimed that his message came straight from heaven (see Revelation 1:11), and he even added this curse to anyone who tries to add to or subtract from Scripture: "I testify to everyone who hears the words of the prophecy of this book: if anyone adds to them, God will add to him the plagues which are written in this book; and if anyone takes away from the words of the book of this prophecy, God will take away his part from the tree of life and from the holy city, which are written in this book" (Revelation 22:18–19).

The Development of the Roman Catholic Canon

Many Christians are aware that the Old Testament of the Roman Catholic Bible contains about a dozen extra books the Protestant church has rejected as not being Scripture. They are called the Apocrypha, which means "secret things" or "secret writings." There are some important reasons for rejecting these books that you need to understand if you are going to interact with your Catholic friends.

One reason these books are in the Catholic Bible is that the Roman church and the Protestant church take a fundamentally different approach to the issue of canonicity. The Catholic position is that the church of Rome determines the canon. What this means is that even though the Hebrew canon does not contain the Apocrypha, and even though Jesus and the apostles never referred to them at all or quoted them, the Catholic Church believes it has the authority to declare these books as Scripture.

But the books of the Apocrypha fail on every criteria for inclusion in the Bible. I mentioned above the most telling arguments against them. The fact that the Jews rejected them is a hugely important witness against them. So is the silence of Jesus and the church on them, and their consistent rejection by the Protestant church over the centuries when the canon was being assembled.

The Apocryphal books also fail the test of internal evidence. They never claim to be the Word of God, and quite frankly much of their content consists of the kind of "Jewish myths" that Paul warned the church to stay away from (Titus 1:14). They also contain serious doctrinal errors, as one of the books teaches that we need to give money to go to heaven.

Now part of the problem with the Catholic view is that the Roman church believes in apostolic succession. This is the view that the authority of the apostles was passed directly from the Twelve to the Roman church, and is still in their hands.

The Catholic Church is not alone in that view, by the way, for the Mormons also make the same claim. But the Bible says that the era of the apostles ended when the last apostle died. How do we know? Because an apostle had to be an eyewitness of Jesus' resurrection (see Acts 1:22). Apostolic succession is not a biblical doctrine.

The Beauty of the Canon

This idea may seem out of place in a heavily doctrinal discussion, but I want to compare God's work collecting the books of Scripture into one magnificent volume to a man picking flowers for his beloved.

The two begin a walk through a garden, and at first the man's beloved has nothing in her hands. But as they go along the path, he keeps picking individual flowers and giving them to her until she comes to the end of the walk holding a fabulous bouquet of sixty-six flowers. Each flower is a work of perfection in itself, and blends perfectly with all the other flowers to form a bouquet of such unsurpassed beauty that any other flower from any other garden would only spoil it.

This is what God did as He walked through the "garden" of history collecting the books of His Word. He directed a well-ordered, clearly defined process by which these books were authenticated. Each book in Scripture meets the rule or canon of the faith, and carries the Holy Spirit's stamp of approval. You don't need to worry that anything good was left out. On the contrary, you can be sure that what you hold in your hands is "the whole purpose of God" (Acts 20:27)—the very Word of God.

THE
BENEFITS
OF
GOD'S WORD

11
THE BIBLE PRODUCES SPIRITUAL LIFE

A cartoon that recently appeared in the comics section of our local Dallas newspaper illustrates a spiritual truth that is extremely relevant to the subject of this chapter.

The cartoon showed a rather confused-looking man lying in bed in the hospital with an IV in his arm. A nurse and smiling doctor are standing next to the man's bed, and the doctor is saying, "Well, we had an unexpected turn of events during your autopsy."

Now I've had people in the funeral business tell me that corpses can twitch and move, but I have never heard of a dead person coming back to life during an autopsy! The reason I mention this cartoon is that it's a pretty good picture of what happened to us when we were dead in our sins and on our way to eternal separation from God in hell.

What happened was that there was an unexpected turn of events during our spiritual autopsy. The heavenly coroner's report that said we were utterly dead and without hope was set aside by the grace of God. The reason is that God brought us back from the dead and gave us spiritual life—and the means He used to awaken us to our need and turn us toward Him was His eternal Word.

Peter said this about the Bible's power to bring new life: "You have been born again not of seed which is perishable but imperishable, that is, through the living and enduring word of God. For, 'All flesh is like grass, and all its glory like the flower of grass. The grass withers, and the flower falls off, but the word of the Lord endures forever.' And this is the word which was preached to you" (1 Peter 1:23–25). God's Word is so powerful it can bring life out of death.

In this section of the book we want to answer the "So what?" question that every preacher ought to address as he delivers a sermon. This is the payoff, so to speak, the part that answers this question in the listeners' minds: "So what? Now that I know this truth, what difference does it make? What should I do about it?"

We have been studying the attributes of God's transforming Word, how it was transmitted and preserved, and the basic principles for understanding God's revelation. Now I want us to consider the blessings or benefits that the Bible holds for people who are willing to pay the price to have a dynamic relationship with God through His Word.

THE WORD OF GOD IS LIFE-GIVING

Talking about the Bible's life-giving power is the right place to start, because no other spiritual benefit would do us any good if we had not been given new life.

When the apostle John wrote his first letter to teach believers how to have intimate fellowship with God, he referred to Jesus Christ as "the Word of Life" (1 John 1:1). John went on to say that this Word was "manifested" (v. 2) to him and the other apostles who saw Jesus in His flesh. We do not have that privilege now, but we have the same Word of Life because we have the completed Bible that embodies and reveals Jesus to us. There is no division or contradiction between the Bible and Jesus Christ, who is also called "the Word" in the first verse of John's gospel. Jesus gives life and His Word gives life because the two operate in concert with each other.

Jesus declared in John 6:63, "The words that I have spoken to you are spirit and are life." Peter responded in that same chapter when everyone but the Twelve had deserted Jesus, "Lord, to whom shall we go? You have words of eternal life" (v. 68). The book of Hebrews reminds us, "The word of God is living" (4:12), and thus it can impart life.

We Were Dead Without the Life-Giving Word

How grateful should we be for the fact that we have been made alive by the imperishable seed of God's Word? We should be eternally grateful, since the news in the divine coroner's report was as bad as it gets. This is what God said about us before we were saved: "You were dead in your transgressions and sins" (Ephesians 2:1 NIV).

This is a chapter about life, so we don't want to dwell too long on the subject of death. But the blessing of spiritual life only shines in all of its glory when we see it against the dark backdrop of the spiritual death that had us in its grip. Besides, all of us have family members or friends who are still living in the realm of spiritual death, and we need to be reminded of their desperate condition to spur us to reach out to them with God's life-giving Word.

Probably the hardest thing for unbelievers to grasp is that outside of Jesus Christ, they are dead. Not just a little bit ill or even barely alive, but as dead now as they will be throughout eternity apart from God's saving grace.

The reason it is so hard for non-Christians to get their minds around the reality of spiritual death is that they don't feel or act dead, and neither do other unbelievers around them. They walk, talk, go to work every day, raise their families, and do other things that living people do.

But the truth is that people without God are like the zombies in those old horror movies with titles like "Night of the Living Dead." You see, these people are coming out of their graves and moving around, terrorizing folk because they are looking for something they don't have, which is life. And they cannot find life because they are living in the realm of death.

This is the real condition of lost people. They are the living dead because death in Scripture is separation, never mere cessation of existence. We will never stop existing, for our souls and spirits are immortal. The problem most unbelievers have is that they don't understand the Bible's definition of death. Of course, the Bible recognizes physical death as the moment when the body is separated from the soul and spirit. But the Bible's overriding concern is with spiritual death, in which the unsaved already exist, and which will become irrevocable when they die and are separated from God forever. For lost people, physical death is the entrance into eternal or spiritual death.

When Adam and Eve rebelled against God, His earlier warning became their death sentence. God had told Adam not to eat from the forbidden tree in Eden, saying, "In the day that you eat from it you will surely die" (Genesis 2:17). And the day Adam and Eve ate from it, they died spiritually—that is, they were separated from God and cut off from the source of true life, which is found in intimate relationship and fellowship with God.

Adam and Eve continued to live, and they certainly looked alive to each other and to those around them. But they were spiritually dead people in physically alive bodies. We can see this crucial distinction in Jesus' word to a would-be disciple who wanted to wait until his father died before following Jesus: "Allow the dead to bury their own dead; but as for you, go and proclaim everywhere the kingdom of God" (Luke 9:60).

In other words, Jesus told this man to let the spiritually dead bury their physical dead. The Lord wasn't being coldhearted, but He knew that if this man went back to live in that realm of spiritual death from which he had come, he would succumb to his environment and not follow Jesus. There is another example of the difference between physical and spiritual life in Paul's statement about a person who abandons dependence on God to go in search of physical pleasure: "But she who gives herself to wanton pleasure is dead even while she lives" (1 Timothy 5:6).

Jesus Came to Give Us Abundant Life

The classic statement of God's life-giving purpose for us is in John 10:10. Jesus said, "I came that they may have life, and have it abundantly." Notice that Jesus does not just give life, but multiplies it into abundant, overflowing life. We could paraphrase John 10:10 as, "I came that they might live—and I mean really live!" And we know from 1 Peter 1:23 that the means God uses to give us abundant life is His eternal Word.

Moses told the people of Israel just before they went into the Promised Land, "Take to your heart all the words with which I am warning you today. . . . For it is not an idle word for you; indeed it is your life. And by this word you will prolong your days in the land" (Deuteronomy 32:46–47).

Israel needed to understand that God's Word was not a nice addition to their lives, but absolutely necessary for their lives. Jesus understood the power of the Word, which is why He told Satan in the wilderness, "Man shall not live on bread alone, but on every word that proceeds out of the mouth of God" (Matthew 4:4). Real life is found in God's Word, not in the things that we can touch, taste, see, hear, and smell.

Most people miss the abundant life God promises because they look for life in the physical realm. But all that material things can do is provide people with more camouflage to hide the fact that they are dead and empty on the inside. What I mean is that a person can buy a lot of toys and nice clothes and good times that may bring temporary enjoyment and keep him from thinking about how dead he feels deep within. But even other people can't fill a person's spiritual emptiness.

There is only one place and Person we can look to for real life.

Jesus prayed on the night before His crucifixion, "This is eternal life, that they may know You, the only true God, and Jesus Christ whom You have sent" (John 17:3). This verse makes it clear that life is found in knowing God through Jesus—and we know this message of life because it is recorded in God's Word.

Christians like to talk and sing about the golden streets and the mansions of heaven, but those are the side benefits, the perks. The essence of heaven is the uninterrupted knowledge of God. Think of it as getting to know God without having to endure any commercials.

Television advertisers know to place their commercials right at the best part of the program to keep you coming back. But heaven will be commercial free, praise God! And the story will keep getting better and unfolding every second because God is infinite and there is no end to His perfections. As glorious as it is to see the revelation of God in Scripture, imagine what it will be like to see Him face-to-face.

Now let me ask you something before we move on. If the gold and the mansions of heaven are the bonus up there, the side benefits compared to knowing God, shouldn't the same thing be true for us here on earth? All of the stuff we sometimes cling to so hard is just a temporary loan from God to get us by until we are with Him forever. Don't get confused about the source of abundant life. It is found only in a relationship with God, and the Bible is the only Word that can deliver that life to you.

The world would have us believe that we are in the land of the living on our way to the land of the dying. But nothing could be further from the truth. We are in the land of the dying on our way to the land of the living.

But even in the world of the dying, God says you can be among the living because of what His Word can do. Even if everyone around you is dying, you can be fully alive. I like how Paul puts it: "Though our outer man is decaying, yet our inner man is being renewed day by day" (2 Corinthians 4:16). Our bodies may be accumulating wrinkles and gray hair at a faster pace than we would like, and we may move slower today than we ever did before. But at the same time, our inner person should be getting younger every day as we are renewed by the Holy Spirit using the Word of God.

So if you are getting older on the outside and older on the inside, you are two times old! You should be getting younger and fresher spiritually, not older. If you are not getting younger as a Christian on the inside, don't blame God or His Word. It is alive and continually fresh.

THE BIBLE GIVES EVIDENCE OF BEING ALIVE

The consistent testimony of the Bible's authors is that the Word they wrote is alive and has the ability to produce life in anyone who will receive it. God's witness to His Word is the most important proof of its life-giving power. But there are other proofs that provide validating evidence that the Word of God is alive.

The Word of God Has Given Life to Millions

One of these proofs is the legions of Christians throughout the ages who have found new life as the Spirit applied the Word to their lives (see James 1:18). Only living things can produce life. Inanimate objects do not have the ability to bring life out of nothing, as God did when He spoke creation into existence with His Word. Neither can inanimate objects bring life out of death, as God does through His Word whenever a person is born again.

The Word of God Is Eternally Fresh

Another evidence of the Bible's life is its incredible, inexhaustible freshness. I have been preaching for about thirty years, and in some ways I feel as if I am just beginning to understand the Bible. I have not even begun to explore all of its depths, and I am confident that any other biblically based pastor would say the same thing.

It is impossible to imagine studying any other book for decades, and preaching from it every week, without exhausting both yourself and your hearers. But the Bible is preached, taught, read, and otherwise examined in detail thousands of times every week across the world, and no one has ever been able to say, "OK, that's it. I've covered the whole Bible and there's nothing left to say about it."

Sometimes we hear about people who get hooked on a series of books or movies, and devour every detail. Some watch a particular film or film series so many times they can recite every word of the dialogue and answer the most minute question about any scene. When the film *Stars Wars* was first released, a boy who had watched it hundreds of times compiled a book of trivia questions related to the film that became a big seller. The film trilogy *The Lord of the Rings* has also generated this kind of fanatic devotion.

But let me give you a challenge. Try getting several hundred people together, or several dozen for that matter, and ask them to meet at least once on Sunday and again on Wednesday night for the rest of their lives to study, expound, and discuss any popular book or movie, or any combination thereof. I'll guarantee you that it won't last long, because after a while even the most die-hard fanatic will get sick of talking about the same material over and over again.

Yet despite the fact that the Bible is thousands of years old, millions of people are still gathering every week to study, expound, and discuss this amazing Book. How anyone can claim that the Bible is just another piece of writing is beyond me. That doesn't even make sense, given the overwhelming evidence that the Bible is alive. The Bible declares of itself, "The grass withers, the flower fades, but the word of our God stands forever" (Isaiah 40:8).

I realize I may be "preaching to the choir" as I share these things with you. But I also know that you probably have times when the Bible doesn't *seem* to be alive. Your theology may tell you the Word is living and active, but there are times when it seems that the Word is not doing anything in you. It appears to have lost its freshness.

The most important thing I can say to this is that the Word is alive and active, even when it doesn't seem so to us. The problem may be that we are in a winter season in our lives in which it appears that everything is dead.

If you are in a winter season right now, don't forget that even though the leaves fall off the trees and the grass turns brown in winter (at least here in Texas), the appearance of death is just that—only an appearance. When spring comes, those trees and lawns that seemed to be dead and gone last winter will burst into life.

In the same way, the Bible does not lose its life. You may be looking at your Bible today and seeing no signs of life, but be assured that the life is there. The best thing you can do is stay in the Word until the winter is past and God's revelation bursts forth with new life in your heart.

What most Christians do when they are experiencing the coldness and deadness of winter in their inner beings is push away the Word because it isn't "working" for them. However, when we do this we cut ourselves off from the very source of the life we need so badly.

I turn off my lawn sprinklers whenever it rains to save money. But sometimes I forget to turn them back on, and in the heat and dryness of a Texas summer I look outside one day and see that, all of a sudden, my green grass is turning brown. It is heading toward death because it is not being watered, and the blazing sun is baking it dry. The grass is withering because it has nothing to give it life. But when I turn the sprinkler system back on and the life-giving water flows regularly, the grass becomes green again.

There are a lot of brown Christians—brown in attitude, not in complexion. They are shriveling up because the Word is not flowing in their hearts, and the world, the flesh, and the devil are baking them dry. They forgot to turn the sprinklers back on. They forgot to develop a dynamic relationship with the living God as His Holy Spirit administers His Word to them (see 1 Peter 1:24–25).

The Word of God Makes Things Grow

Another evidence that the Bible is alive is that it produces growth. "Therefore, putting aside all malice and all deceit and hypocrisy and envy and all slander, like newborn babies, long for the pure milk of the word, so that by it you may grow in respect to salvation" (1 Peter 2:1–2).

At the time of the writing of this book, my youngest grandson was seven months old. He had spent most of his life up to that point drinking milk, which produced amazing growth in his body. Part of the reason for this growth was his absolute dedication to his milk. Every few hours he demanded milk, and woe be to anyone who thwarted that desire. My grandson had an insatiable, God-given thirst for the very thing that would help him grow, and he wasn't satisfied with anything else.

Someone may say, "I wish the Bible had that kind of attraction for me and was producing growth in my heart."

Why is it that growth doesn't take place in some believers' lives, if the Word is capable of producing growth and God wants us to grow? As I was thinking about this, the answer hit me in verse 1 of our text. We tend to read over it quickly to get to the part about growing by the milk of the Word. But look again at 1 Peter 2:1. Here is a list of "dirty laundry" we need to do something about— sins and poor attitudes that we have to rid ourselves of before the milk of the Word can flow freely and provide its nourishment.

Some people say to me, "Pastor, I don't know what's wrong. I read my Bible every day. I go to church on Sunday and Wednesday. I read Christian books, listen to Christian radio, and watch Christian television. But I still feel spiritually weak, like I'm not getting what I need to grow."

The answer could be that these believers are not removing the hindrances to their growth. Feeding on the "junk food" of sin kills our legitimate hunger for the Word. The problem for many non-growing Christians is not that they need more Bible study or the latest book on spiritual growth. Their biggest need is for some spiritual dialysis.

Our kidneys are designed to purify our blood by removing the waste so the blood can carry the proper nourishment to the rest of the body. But when our kidneys cease to function, the waste in the blood does not get cleansed and it poisons the body.

If you are in need of kidney dialysis, it does not matter how much healthy food you eat. The quality of your diet becomes irrelevant because there is no filtering of the impurities, and the best diet in the world won't keep you alive when your kidneys are not functioning properly.

The same is true in our spiritual lives. If the impurities of sin are not cleansed by the blood of Christ, don't be surprised if you don't experience growth even though you may be reading your Bible regularly and going to church.

I don't like the taste, the smell, or even the sight of fish, which means I don't like to see fish lying next to any food I plan to eat. For me, putting fish alongside my food is asking the good stuff to hang out with the bad stuff. And when that happens, the bad stuff makes the good stuff taste bad.

The reason the Bible doesn't taste like good stuff to some people is that they are putting the bad stuff alongside the Word, which spoils its goodness for them. They are not growing by the pure milk of the Word because that pure milk is being spoiled by sin. But when sin is addressed, the nourishment of Scripture produces growth (see 1 Timothy 4:6).

The Word of God Has Unbelievable Power

We also know the Word of God is alive because of its power. People who had no relationship to God and knew nothing of His grace have picked up a Bible, begun reading it, and fallen on their faces crying out for God's mercy and grace. Then they have testified that whereas they were dead in their sins, they are now alive in Jesus Christ. The last time I checked, no other book has this life-changing, life-giving power. The testimony of those who have been transformed by God's Word is that the Bible is the only Book that reads you as you read it. But sometimes we don't like the Bible's power because it makes us uncomfortable by slicing us open, as Hebrews 4:12 says, and exposing our deepest thoughts and attitudes. It works the other way too, and there is nothing like the

excitement of reading a passage that has your name on it as the Holy Spirit speaks directly to you through the Word. But whether the Bible convicts or confirms you, you are experiencing its power.

Satan knows where the power is, which is why he will do anything to keep you from the Word. If my cell phone is detached from its power source for too long, it becomes weak and eventually will quit altogether. Then I can't hear from the people I need to be in communication with. When you have been detached from your spiritual power source too long, you don't hear from God. You want to hear His voice, but you can't because you have been doing your own thing too long.

YOU CAN TAP INTO THE BIBLE'S LIFE-GIVING POWER

It wouldn't be fair to talk about the Bible's ability to produce life without helping you tap into this life. There is a very important verse that gives us three basic ways we can use and enjoy the power of God's Word: "Blessed is he who reads and those who hear the words of the prophecy, and heed the things which are written in it" (Revelation 1:3).

Everybody wants to be blessed, which means to be full, satisfied, and happy. John said that the state of being blessed that we seek comes when we read, "seed," and heed God's Word.

You Need to Read the Word

We don't need to say much here, because we have already talked about the importance of reading the Bible on a systematic basis. There are many daily reading plans available that will take you through the entire Bible in one year. Someone has calculated that if we would cut out one thirty-minute television program per day and devote that time to the Word, we could read through the Bible twice in one year.

I hate to keep bringing up the subject of food, but the fact is

that most people don't let a day go by without eating. We will even go out of our way to find food when we are hungry. We will gladly forego a thirty-minute television program to pick up a knife and fork when our stomachs are growling.

A guy told me recently that when he and his wife drove to north Dallas to refinance their home, he got lost because he thought he knew where the mortgage company was and so he didn't ask the person on the phone for the address or directions. The couple had the paperwork with them, so naturally the guy's wife asked him, "Did you read these papers to see if the address is in here?"

"Yes," he said, "but the only address I saw was their Denver office." Now every married man knows where this is heading! His wife read the papers while he was driving around in circles getting evangelically ticked off, and she found the mortgage company's Dallas address prominently listed on about page 6. All he had done was quickly scan the cover sheet because he didn't think he needed to read everything.

You Need to "Seed" the Word

Revelation 1:3 promises a blessing to those who "hear" the Word of God. I call this "seeding" the Word because in biblical terms, hearing doesn't mean simply letting the words of Scripture penetrate your consciousness. It means internalizing what God tells you, letting the Word take root in your heart like a seed that produces a harvest.

This is why Jesus said on more than one occasion, "He who has ears to hear, let him hear" (Matthew 11:15). This statement would not make sense were it not for the fact that it is possible for us to hear something without letting it get down inside of us. But to really hear the Word is to say, "Dear God, I'm reading, so please talk to me." If you develop that mind-set as you read your Bible or sit under its teaching, you'll hear, because now you're asking God to speak to you, and you're ready to really listen.

The biblical word for this process is *meditation* (see Psalms 1:2; 19:14; 104:34). Just as grass has to absorb the rain into the ground in order to benefit from it, we must absorb God's Word into our deepest being by meditating on its meaning and applying it to our lives. We must believe God has something to say to us, and be listening. Your Bible study will take on a whole new dimension when you hear the Word as you are reading it or as it is being taught to you. Mighty things happen when God's Word is allowed to make itself at home in us (see Colossians 3:16).

You Need to Heed the Word

The third requirement for the blessing God promised in Revelation 1:3 is to heed, or obey, the Word. "Prove yourselves doers of the word, and not merely hearers who delude themselves" (James 1:22). Now don't be thrown off by this statement about hearing the Word. The key is "merely," meaning those who let the Word go in one ear and out the other without taking seed.

Some people read the Bible but don't hear it because the Word doesn't "register" with them. Others read and hear the Word, but don't get up and obey it. Some don't do any of these—but the blessing comes in doing all three.

I encourage you to read Jesus' parable of the sower in Luke 8:4–15. It might better be called the parable of the seeds, because Jesus' point was how the good seed of His Word was received by four kinds of soil, representing human hearts. The soil "beside the road" (v. 5) is the heart that rejects the seed outright. The rocky soil is the heart that receives the seed but doesn't do anything to nurture it, and so it withers away. The soil that is full of weeds pictures those people who receive the seed and may have all good intentions of growing, but the cares and worries of this life sprout up and choke out the seed. These are the folk who leave church on Sunday shouting glory, but fade out on Monday as life bogs them down.

But when the seed of the Word takes root in a heart that's pursuing God, you're going to reap a harvest. Things you have been trying to change for years are going to change as God works within you.

My clothes are fitting better lately because I am cutting out sweets, eating more vegetables and fruits, and working out. When I changed my diet, it changed me. And let me tell you something, when you get a taste of positive change you want to keep it going. When you get a taste of what it feels like to be really alive, you want to live more. Get yourself a good taste of God's life-giving Word, and you will develop an appetite that won't be satisfied with anything else as you continue to be "transformed into the same image [of God] from glory to glory" (2 Corinthians 3:18) by the power of God's Word.

12

THE BIBLE PROVIDES SPIRITUAL DIRECTION

Former baseball star and dugout philosopher Yogi Berra is well known for his uncomplicated advice to someone seeking the right direction in life: "When you come to the fork in the road, take it."

A lot of people wish life's decisions were that easy. No issue hits us more often as we seek to live the Christian life and please the Lord than what we should do and which way we should go in any given situation. We need godly direction and guidance for everything from the choice of a mate to the choice of a school or career. We also need help with financial decisions that can affect our families for years to come.

Yogi Berra was right about one thing. When you come to a fork in the road, you have to take one path or the other. We are faced with many forks in the road that can perplex us, but thankfully, another benefit of Scripture is that it gives us sound direction for all of life.

Our need for God's guidance is nothing new. Throughout the

Bible, God's people cried out for His help when they were either at a fork in the road or had their backs against the wall. Moses and the Israelites were trapped between the Red Sea and the Egyptian army in Exodus 14 when God told them to move forward into the sea. He commanded Moses to stretch his staff out over the water. Solomon prayed as he assumed the throne of Israel, "I am but a little child; I do not know how to go out or come in" (1 Kings 3:7). Solomon then asked for wisdom to guide God's people.

I'm sure you know what it feels like to be in an "I don't know what to do" dilemma. There are situations in which you simply don't know which way to go. At times like this you need a light to guide you, which makes the psalmist's ancient statement of God's guidance very relevant for us today: "Your word is a lamp to my feet and a light to my path" (Psalm 119:105). The Bible shows us the direction we should take. We do not have to wander aimlessly in the fog of human opinion.

GOD'S GUIDANCE IS PERSONAL AND SPECIFIC

One of the first things that stands out about this great verse is how personal and specific the guidance is that we receive from God's Word. We can see this, for instance, in the psalmist's use of the word *lamp.*

Watch Each Step You Take

Lamps in biblical days were a far cry from the kind of lighting we have today. Our lights can illuminate an entire room or a large area. And if we are walking in the dark, we have flashlights that can really brighten up the path and show us any hidden obstacles.

But in biblical days a small oil lamp was a personal item, providing only enough light for a person to see the next step as he walked, or to illuminate a small corner of a room. So a person walking along a path had to go deliberately, watching each step. This is true of so many decisions and choices in life. Rarely if ever do we see an entire issue in one grand moment of illumination and know instantly everything to do. God has designed life in such a way that we have to trust Him one step at a time, and so the Bible's assurance is that He will give us light for the next step.

The lamp we are talking about had much the same effect as the lamps that miners wear on their hard hats when they go down into the darkness of the mines. Each miner's lamp illuminates his own path and helps him see which way to go, and the psalmist says the Bible is a light that enables us to see the right course to take.

Find Guidance from God

The first-person pronouns of Psalm 119:105 also reveal that this issue of guidance is personal. It's amazing how one Christian can open the Word and find clear guidance, while another can read the same passage and see nothing. This is true even though all believers have the same Bible and the same Holy Spirit. God does not play favorites, but He reveals Himself to those who seek Him with all their hearts (see Jeremiah 29:13). Two Christians can be very different in their sensitivity to the Spirit and His ministry of illuminating the Word.

Spiritual direction works something like the passenger reading-lights in airplanes. Each passenger's light is focused directly over his or her seat so as not to shine in the faces of the other passengers in the row. If you want to see what you're doing, you have to use the light that is provided specifically for you. You can't borrow someone else's light for your purposes. Just to carry the analogy through, every passenger has the same kind of light available, so no one can say the airline is unfair or playing favorites.

The personal nature of spiritual guidance is another testimony to the fact that God wants to have a deeply personal and intimate relationship with you through His Word. That's why when you come to the Word each day, you want to ask, "Lord, what do You want to say to me today? What do You have for me?" The Holy Spirit has a unique word of guidance for you given your unique personality, background, and situation.

Now let me add that not all of God's guidance is unique to each believer. By this I mean that all of us are obligated to obey the clear commands of His Word that apply to everyone and that guide us away from sin and toward a life of holiness. There is a world of difference between seeking God's direction for a marriage partner or a difficult decision and saying that God has "led" you to make a decision that flatly contradicts His revealed truth.

But within this biblical framework of guidance, God's Word still encourages us individually to seek God's mind and will for every area of our lives. You can benefit from the wisdom of other believers, and I encourage you to find and follow godly mentors who have been down the road ahead of you. But you cannot live off of someone else's relationship with God in terms of what the Holy Spirit wants to say to you.

FIND DIRECTION AND BLESSING IN GOD'S WORD

Why is it so important that the Bible be the source we go to first for our spiritual guidance and decision making? Because God has only promised to bless His Word, not our own ideas or the opinions of others.

Be Careful of Counselors

Now please don't think that I am putting down human counselors. As a pastor, I have spent literally thousands of hours seeking to help married couples, families, and individuals work through problems, make decisions, and find God's best for their lives. What I am saying is that any counselor or adviser who does not anchor that counsel in God's Word is suspect, because "the foolishness of God is wiser than men, and the weakness of God is stronger than men" (1 Corinthians 1:25).

Beware of the Enemy's Fortresses

There is another reason we need the wisdom and guidance found only in God's Word. This has to do with the nature of our human mind and the way it has been corrupted by sin. We have a serious problem when it comes to figuring out what we should do and where we should go. Paul explained this dilemma in a crucial passage of Scripture:

> For though we walk in the flesh, we do not war according to the flesh, for the weapons of our warfare are not of the flesh, but divinely powerful for the destruction of fortresses. We are destroying speculations and every lofty thing raised up against the knowledge of God, and we are taking every thought captive to the obedience of Christ. (2 Corinthians 10:3–5)

This is spiritual warfare language, which may seem out of place in a discussion of spiritual guidance. But not in this case, because there is someone out there who does not want you and me to find God's direction.

You know what a fortress looks like with its high, seemingly impenetrable walls. The problem we face in seeking God's direction for life is that we have a formidable enemy called the devil whose job is to erect fortresses in our minds. These are things such as ungodly and unbiblical ways of thinking, ingrained habits and attitudes, or even addictions that keep us from hearing from God and finding His will.

Now if you are on the path seeking God's direction and you come up against a fortress blocking your way, it has to come down before you can move on. But it will only fall if you use the right weapons, which are spiritual and include things like the Word, prayer, and fasting.

The reason many of the fortresses in our lives are not falling is that we are using the wrong weapons. The devil loves it when you try to overcome these things in the power of the flesh, because he has you on his turf now. He operates best when we are in the realm of the flesh, and we are no match for him.

Paul said that although we live in the flesh, we do not operate by the flesh. But as I have suggested, far too many Christians do exactly that—operate by the flesh, or by human reasoning, wisdom, or willpower. You'll never tear down fortresses of thought and habit simply by getting another human viewpoint. You have to come at them using the armor of God, which includes the sword of His Word (see Ephesians 6:13–17).

WATCH OUT FOR THE ENEMY'S PARTITIONS

Paul also said we need to destroy speculations and every "lofty thing" that is raised up against the knowledge of God. We need to resist and tear down anything that hinders our ability to get God's viewpoint. The Greek word translated "lofty thing" is very interesting. It refers to a partition, or even an obstacle.

We have a number of rooms in our church that can be divided when necessary by movable partitions. A partition divides one room into two so that it has a "split personality," so to speak. Two classes or meetings can be conducted in the same room because it has been divided.

There's nothing wrong with dividing a room using a partition, but it's another story altogether when we are talking about dividing our minds. We have all known Christians who tried to serve God with a divided mind. What happens is that the devil sets up his partition and it becomes an obstacle to spiritual wholeness because the person is now a spiritual schizophrenic with two sides competing for his attention.

The apostle James had another word for a Christian with a partitioned or divided mind. He called it being "double-minded" (James 1:8), and here's the problem with that. Back in verse 7 James said, "That man ought not to expect that he will receive anything from the Lord." James was saying, "Get rid of your schizophrenia. Stop trying to go two ways at one time if you want to hear from God."

If you are seeking God's direction but also holding out for your own way, you are going to be confused and come up empty as far as direction from God is concerned. Just as fortresses of wrong thinking must be torn down, the partitions that divide our thinking must be destroyed so there is nothing blocking God's Spirit from revealing His wisdom and will to us.

The Bible is talking about Christians in these texts, just in case you were wondering. It is possible for true believers to get so messed up in their minds that they become badly disoriented and hardly give any evidence of being born again.

Let God's Word Be "At Home" in You

So how do we tear down the devil's fortresses and destroy the Berlin Walls of partition that he builds in our minds? Paul gave us the answer: "Let the word of Christ richly dwell within you, with all wisdom teaching and admonishing one another with psalms and hymns and spiritual songs, singing with thankfulness in your hearts to God" (Colossians 3:16).

Comparing this passage to its parallel in Ephesians 5:18–21 reveals that letting God's Word dwell in us is a synonym for being "filled with the Spirit" (Ephesians 5:18). This is important because when we talk about the Word doing this or that in our lives, we are talking about the Holy Spirit's ministry of making the Word real to us. When the Holy Spirit fills a person, He brings with Him the Word.

The key word in Colossians 3 is *dwell,* which means to let the Spirit and the Word of God make themselves at home in your heart. Far too many times God is not really at home, even in a Christian's heart. And you know what it's like when you don't feel at home or feel welcome in someone's house. You find it very hard to relax, and you don't feel comfortable talking about anything of real depth or intimacy. The person who wants God's direction must let His Word move in and go wherever He wants it to go in the house.

How do you make God's Word at home in your heart? The same way you make people feel at home in your house. You say to God, "My home is Your home." Letting the Word be at home is saying to God, "Lord, I throw open the doors of my life to You. Show me whatever it is You want me to do." This is the same concept as being filled with the Holy Spirit, which Paul compared to being controlled by alcohol. A person who is drunk is under the control of alcohol so completely that he may talk nonsense and we say, "That was the liquor talking." That's the level of control the Spirit wants to exercise within us through the Word. God wants to do the talking.

Let God's Word Do the Talking

When you have this attitude of submission to God fixed in your mind, then you are ready for Colossians 3:17, which says, "Whatever you do in word or deed, do all in the name of the Lord Jesus, giving thanks through Him to God the Father."

We have to understand that God's direction comes as His Word permeates our minds. Do you want to know God's will for you? Then heed Romans 12:2, "Be transformed by the renewing of your mind, so that you may prove what the will of God is, that which is good and acceptable and perfect." To renew your mind is to change your thinking, which is vital because every decision in life is related to the way you think. There is no choice without thought.

Our problem too often is that we want to do all the talking. We think we already have all the information we need to make an informed decision without having to consult God's Word for guidance. In other words, we think we are smart enough to make it on our own, at least with this one decision. But thinking that we can collect all the data we need on our own is an illusion.

Folk get their college degree, go on for a master's, and then, Lord have mercy, they get a Ph.D. and nobody can talk to them. But people who think they have life figured out and don't need God's help are like those of whom Paul said, "[They are] always learning and never able to come to the knowledge of the truth" (2 Timothy 3:7). Now given that we are not as smart as we think, wouldn't it be better to seek the counsel of our all-knowing, all-powerful, and all-seeing God? The way to do that is to let His Word saturate your mind.

There is another choice, but it's not pretty. "The mind set on the flesh [or human viewpoint] is death, but the mind set on the

Spirit is life and peace" (Romans 8:6). That's about as clear as God can make it. This is the difference between a defeated Christian and a victorious Christian; between a frustrated single person and a fulfilled single person; between a marriage that makes it and one that doesn't; between an addiction that won't go away and one that we gain victory over. God has some incredible guidance for the person whose mind is set on Him. But when we raise up a partition, we block the flow of His divine direction to our minds.

GET TUNED IN TO THE
FREQUENCY OF THE WORD

There is a Dallas radio station I like to listen to whenever I drive south to see my son Jonathan at Baylor University in Waco. But the farther I get away from Dallas, the more the reception starts to fade. It's frustrating because the station will go out for a second and then fade back in, and I get the next snippet of the program or song I was enjoying. But just when I think I am locked in on the signal again, it fades out. Or even worse, I start picking up other frequencies and hear voices coming in from other stations that I didn't want to hear.

Messing with the station settings doesn't help, either, because I'm too far from the broadcast signal to receive it. Of course, my station comes in stronger and stronger as I head back toward Dallas, because now I am going toward the signal instead of away from it.

The question for those of us who want God's direction in life is: Are we moving toward the frequency of His Spirit, or away from it? If you are moving away from intimacy with and obedience to God, and if your mind is distracted by other voices on other frequencies, don't be surprised if your decisions start looking confusing and you aren't hearing much from heaven.

When we use partitions at church to divide a room, the sound from one class is muted so the class on the other side of the divider is not disturbed. That arrangement may be good for classes, but it's not good for living. God doesn't want the devil on the other side of your mind, as it were, conducting his class while the Lord is trying to get His Word through to you.

Let God's Word Guide You Safely

The Word of God is meant to be a lamp and a light for you. To what end? Psalm 119:133 tells us: "Establish my footsteps in Your word, and do not let any iniquity have dominion over me." Your footsteps—your thinking, choices, and decisions—must be grounded in the Bible so you will not be controlled by sin. In order for an airplane to land safely and arrive at the proper gate at the terminal, at least three things must happen. First, an air-traffic controller must maintain contact with the plane and give the pilot clearance and instructions to land. Second, if the landing is at night, the runway lights must be lit to guide the pilot down onto the right runway. And third, once the plane is on the ground the guy with the red batons must guide the plane to the right parking spot at its gate.

The same thing is true in being directed by God. God must be able to stay in contact with you, so He can tell you when it's safe to land. Then, you need the illumination of His Word to show you where to land. And you need the Spirit to show you the specific parking spot where you need to stop. You need these three—God, His Word, and His Spirit—working in harmony to show you where to go.

You say, "But Tony, the Bible doesn't deal with my specific situation." But that's not true. Now I acknowledge that the Bible does not give you the name of the person you should marry, or the name of the company where you should work. Those are really side issues, however. The Bible does deal with your situation, because whether you are looking for a job or a mate, the Bible has very specific guidance for you.

For instance, the Bible says concerning marriage, "Do not be bound together with unbelievers" (2 Corinthians 6:14). So you already know whom you should marry—a fellow believer in Christ. The Bible also says, "Abstain from sexual immorality" (1 Thessalonians 4:3), and "Marriage is to be held in honor among all, and the marriage bed is to be undefiled" (Hebrews 13:4). So now you know how to behave with the Christian you marry and toward everyone else who is not your spouse. And the Bible tells wives to submit to their husbands, and husbands to love their wives the way Christ loves the church (see Ephesians 5:22–33), so now you know how to please Christ in your marriage, which is even more important than the person you marry.

Those are a lot of specifics, and we could add more. So you are all set to get married as soon as you find someone who fits this description and is committed to Christ and to you.

Now I know that what you want is a name—and I'm willing to admit that the guidelines above are general for all Christians. But think about it. When you go to apply God's Word to your situation, His guidance is not general at all, but very specific to you. This is where the Holy Spirit comes in. His job is to take the principles that are true for all believers and use them to give you a lamp to your feet and a light to your path so you can see where *you* should go.

And when you meet someone you are thinking about marrying, the Spirit will shine His light on your decision if you seek Him with all your heart. But for that to happen, the Spirit and the Word must be at home in your heart, as we just saw in Colossians 3:16. So we have come full circle.

Let the Great Physician Give You a Checkup

If you haven't memorized Psalm 37:4, you should. David wrote, "Delight yourself in the Lord; and He will give you the desires of your heart." When your thinking and heart and desires are in agreement with God and His Word, you will hear from Him, because now you both have the same desires. And you have nothing to fear from God's desires, because He wants to give you His best even more than you want to receive it.

With a promise like this on the floor, I have to wonder why so many Christians run away from God's will for them and try to find their own way. These believers do with God's will what a lot of us do when we are sick. Instead of going to the doctor to get the proper diagnosis and treatment, we run to the drugstore and get an over-the-counter medication that may only treat the symptoms.

There are a lot of "over-the-counter" Christians out there. The tragedy of this is that after weeks and weeks of self-treatment, these folks ought to know that their remedies are not doing the job and get themselves to the doctor. After messing up decision after decision and constantly finding themselves running into dead ends, you would think some Christians would realize that self-made decisions are not the solution to their problem. Something else is going on here.

Now imagine taking your store-bought medicines to the doctor and saying, "Fix me up, Doc, but use these medicines. I don't want to use what you might prescribe because I'm afraid it's going to cost me too much. Besides, I've kind of gotten used to being my own doctor."

A doctor will never accept that line. He will put you under his X-ray machine or whatever else is needed to get underneath the surface and look deep inside for the problem.

God won't accept our line either. We can't bring Him our degrees, self-help formulas, lucky rabbits' feet, or other human means for finding direction and say, "Show me the way, Lord, but use these. I don't want to have to dig into Your Word and take Your prescription."

God wants to x-ray our inner being using His Word until our hearts are "open and laid bare to the eyes of Him with whom we have to do" (Hebrews 4:13). Only when we get the true diagnosis can we be fixed up so that the decisions we make are the ones God wants us to make. If we don't give the Great Physician permission to examine our hearts, all we really do when we read His Word or go to church is take an over-the-counter medicine.

Make Sure You Listen to The Right Voice

Our professional basketball team, the Dallas Mavericks, has a little game they play with the fans during halftime or a timeout. They bring somebody down on the floor, blindfold him, and put him on his hands and knees. Then they place a valuable prize somewhere on the floor and the blindfolded person has only so much time to find it. The crowd gets to participate by trying to guide the person to the prize. The crowd is supposed to cheer as the person moves toward the prize, and boo if he moves away from it.

The contestant rarely finds the prize, because the arena floor is large and it's tough to get your bearings when you're blindfolded and thousands of people are screaming at you. But on top of these disadvantages, some fans think it is great fun to boo when the person is actually moving toward the prize to throw him off. In other words, there are deceivers in the crowd to mess up the person seeking guidance, who is already handicapped by his limitations.

Do you see where I'm going? Without God's help, we sinful human beings are already blindfolded and down on our hands and knees groping around trying to find the right way in life. And if we listen to all the voices around us, we'll be even more confused and messed up, because some of those voices are coming from the deceiver Satan and his henchmen.

What we need is someone to take us by the hand and lead us in the way we should go. And we'll find that guiding hand when we reach out our hands and pick up our Bibles. You've got to open the Book and look intently into the Word, which James called "the law of liberty" (James 1:25). The benefit of doing this is found in the last part of the verse, "This man will be blessed in what he does."

But as I suggested earlier, many Christians don't want to make the effort to search the Word. They want an easy, quick answer, even if they have to pay someone for it.

People like this remind me of folks who call information at the telephone company to get a number, even though they know it's available for free in the phone book. They simply don't want to take the time to open the book and work their way through it to get the information they need. They would rather pay someone else to do their looking for them. And now the phone company will even dial the number for an extra fee if the caller wants. I'd be curious to know what percentage of callers opt for this service too. Let's not be Christians who are too lazy to pick up the Book and search out God's wisdom and guidance for ourselves.

The telephone company's information service may occasionally give you a wrong number, as happened to me one time. But God's Spirit will never misdirect you. You will still make mistakes, as we all do, because we are human and fallible. But if we will start with the Bible instead of relying on ourselves and others, we will save ourselves and those close to us a lot of grief and cost—and we will know the joy of hearing God say, "This is the way, walk in it" (Isaiah 30:21).

SOMETIMES WE NEED BIBLICAL COUNSELING

I want to close this chapter by answering an important question that always comes up whenever we talk about the Bible's ability to provide us with the guidance and wisdom we need to live complete, fulfilling lives. The question is this: Does this mean it is unspiritual, or even wrong, for a Christian to seek out a human counselor for help with a serious problem?

People in some Christian circles would answer yes, it is wrong for Christians to go to counselors because these individuals rely too much on human wisdom and the principles of psychology to arrive at their diagnoses and offer solutions. Other Christians would say that there is nothing at all wrong or unspiritual about seeking help for a problem that is beyond the person's ability to handle alone.

The Key Is the Foundation for the Counseling

My advice in this area is between these two poles of absolute rejection and absolute acceptance of the need for counseling. I do not chastise people who need help. We are complex beings made up of body, soul, and spirit (see 1 Thessalonians 5:23), and things can go wrong in our souls and spirits just as they can in our bodies. To condemn somebody for seeking soul healing is like condemning that person for seeking physical healing for an illness or pain.

My concern with this issue is that we had better make sure the counseling we receive is *biblical* counseling. By that I mean far more than the counselor tossing a few Bible verses into the conversation. I am talking about using the Bible as the primary diagnostic tool in getting to the root of the ache in our souls and spirits. The problem with a lot of counseling is that it incorrectly diagnoses the problem because the root issue never gets dealt with.

It reminds me of the old story about the church member who kept asking folks to pray that God would clean out the spider webs in his life. But nothing ever happened, even though he made the same prayer request week after week. But after this had gone on for some time, one brave brother who got tired of the charade cried out in frustration, "Lord, kill that spider!"

One of the things Jesus did for people whose souls were in pain was to "kill the spiders." Think of the woman at the well in John 4. Jesus' meeting with her was not only an evangelistic encounter in which she was saved, but a "counseling session" in which Jesus cut to the heart of her problem: She had gone through five marriages and was living in sin with a man to whom she was not married.

Now someone will object, "Oh sure, that was easy for Jesus to do. He is the all-seeing, all-knowing God." It's true that we cannot see into people's souls the way Jesus could, but that objection misses the point. Jesus has given us His inspired Word that has the power to pierce into our inner beings (as Hebrews 4:12 states so powerfully) and reveal unerringly what is really going on in our deepest hearts.

The problem today is that too much counseling, even Christian counseling, is focused on cleaning out the spider webs in people's lives when God wants to kill the spiders. That's why I say that any counseling that is not deeply embedded in Scripture is ultimately going to be ineffective. Biblical counseling is using the Word of God as the foundation for diagnosing and addressing what people need to know to bring healing to their souls.

The Church Needs to Be a Counseling Center

Talking about biblical counseling usually raises another question, which is, "Great, sounds like just what I or my loved one needs. So where do we find this kind of counseling?"

Obviously, my purpose here is not to provide you with a list of counselors all over America. There are services that help Christians find a believing counselor in their area. But I do want to address a resource for counseling that too many Christians overlook, even though it is actually the first place we should turn. This is the church of Jesus Christ, and in particular, mature believers God has placed in the body who are equipped to counsel others.

Paul told the Romans, "Concerning you, my brethren, I myself also am convinced that you yourselves are full of goodness, filled with all knowledge and able also to admonish one another" (Romans 15:14). This may be the most important verse in Scripture on counseling, because that is exactly what the term *admonish* involves. The Bible says that we are to counsel one another, guided by the Holy Spirit and using the knowledge of God's Word that He has placed within us.

I know that a lot of people will object that this is too simplistic a view of counseling, because people's problems can be very complex and difficult to unravel. But nothing could be further from the truth than to say that mature, godly believers who are filled with the Spirit and God's Word are not competent to counsel others. In fact, God *commands* us to help one another: "Brethren, even if anyone is caught in any trespass, *you who are spiritual,* restore such a one in a spirit of gentleness" (Galatians 6:1, italics added). The best counseling should be in the church, but it's not happening in a lot of cases either because there are not enough spiritually mature people making themselves available, or the church isn't connecting those who need help with those who can help.

Now don't misunderstand. Professional counselors have their place in the body of Christ. My point is that the church has a crucial ministry of counseling to perform that is largely going undone today. We need to raise up a body of mature, godly believers who are equipped to skillfully employ and apply God's truth to other Christians.

If we truly believe that "all Scripture is inspired by God and profitable for teaching, for reproof, for correction, for training in righteousness" (2 Timothy 3:16) and that "His divine power has granted to us everything pertaining to life and godliness" (2 Peter 1:3), then we need to go to the Bible to diagnose, address, and correct the pain in our souls.

13

THE BIBLE BRINGS SPIRITUAL BLESSINGS

When a person goes for a job interview, one of the issues that is sure to come up if the interview process goes far enough is the benefits that come with the job.

Now I wouldn't recommend leading off with this question, or the interview might be very short. But once a company has made it clear what it expects from a potential employee, it's fair for that person to ask about the benefits the job provides. In other words, if you are going to dedicate yourself to your job and give it your best effort day after day, you have the right to ask, "What can I expect to receive from this relationship?"

An employer with a solid benefits program shouldn't mind being asked that question. In fact, God doesn't mind being asked that question by the people He is calling to dedicate their lives for Him. That very question was brought to the floor one day when a rich young man came to Jesus, offering to be His follower. But when Jesus told him to sell everything he had, the man went away severely disappointed (Matthew 19:16–22).

After Jesus made a strong statement about the difficulty of rich people being saved and discussed the issue with the Twelve (vv. 23–26), Peter had a question. Old Pete had been adding stuff up on his calculator and looking at his bank balance, and he came up with zip. So he said to Jesus, "We gave it all up to follow You. What's in this deal for us?" (v. 27, Evans translation).

Now if it were unspiritual for a disciple of Jesus to ask about the rewards of following Him, this would have been a great place for Jesus to severely rebuke Peter and make it clear that anyone who was in this thing for the benefits could go home right now. But instead of chastising Peter, Jesus answered his question: "Truly I say to you . . . everyone who has left houses or brothers or sisters or father or mother or children or farms for My name's sake, will receive many times as much, and will inherit eternal life" (vv. 28–29). Someone said the pay for being a Christian isn't that great, but the retirement plan is out of this world.

So don't apologize for wanting to know about God's benefit plan. It's part of His revealed and recorded Word in places like Psalm 1, which begins, "How blessed." That little phrase means there are incredible benefits for those who take God and His Word seriously. Besides spiritual life and spiritual guidance, the Bible also provides us with spiritual blessings.

It would be almost impossible to get one hundred people to agree on anything. But chances are good that if you asked one hundred people, "Do you want to be blessed?" you would get few if any refusals. I've never met anyone who has told me flat out, "No, Pastor, I really don't want to be blessed." There's something wrong with anyone who doesn't want to be blessed.

Now you *will* get some heavy disagreement if you ask people for their concept of what it means to be blessed. But I'm going to assume you agree with me that when it is all said and done, the only formula for blessing that really matters is God's. So we are going to consider the spiritual benefit of being blessed, according to God's definition in His Word, the only place in which we learn what it means to be truly blessed.

GOD WANTS YOUR BLESSINGS
TO BE MULTIPLIED

Psalm 1:1–3 is a formula for blessing that is both timeless and rich. It doesn't contain any tips on how to get ahead in the stock market or how to land that dream job. What it offers is infinitely better—a pattern for spiritual living that pleases God and opens the treasure stores of heaven.

When You Seek God, You Have Abundant Blessings

The psalmist put the "goodies" right at the front door in these verses. It isn't immediately evident in the English version, but the phrase "how blessed" in verse 1 is a plural word in Hebrew that could be translated, "How many are the blessednesses of. . . ." That may not be very smooth English, but it's great theology! When you seek God, you get blessings multiplied, an abundance of blessings. You roll from one blessing to another.

The Hebrew verb "to be blessed" means basically "to be happy." We all want to be happy, and God wants us to be happy too. It's just that our concept of happiness does not always match His. Biblical happiness is neither the world's idea of happiness as a carefree sail through life with everything coming up roses, nor is it the "name it, claim it" theology of the prosperity teachers who say that God's greatest desire for you is that you be healthy and wealthy.

You Are Blessed When You Enjoy God's Goodness

What does it mean, then, to be blessed or to receive a blessing in the biblical sense? Here is a simple definition: *A blessing is the God-given capacity to enjoy His goodness in your life.*

A lot of people would look at this definition and think it misses the mark. They believe the blessing is the thing itself, not the capacity to enjoy it. In other words, the blessing is good health, the bonus at work, or the big promotion.

Those are certainly nice things to have, but they are not necessarily blessings in the biblical sense. Why? Because there are plenty of people who have all of that, and a whole lot more, and yet aren't enjoying it. That is, they have no sense of God's peace or satisfaction in their hearts, and thus even "good" things can become a source of unhappiness or just drive them to want more.

But when God pours out His goodness to you, He gives you joy and peace and satisfaction with it, regardless of the particular form His goodness may take. Here are two biblical tests you can apply to anything you have or experience that will help you know if it is truly God's blessing, or just the result of your own drivenness.

The first test might be called the peace test. According to Proverbs 10:22, "It is the blessing of the Lord that makes rich, and He adds no sorrow to it." So if you're getting what you want—or working hard to get it—but all you have to show for it is headaches, sleepless nights, and a load of grief, then what you have or what you want is not a blessing from God.

How do you know if you're on the right track? One way to discern this is to compare your pursuit with the weary working man of Ecclesiastes 4:8. This guy didn't even have any dependents to worry about, and yet the Bible says he was working himself to death. "There was no end to all his labor," "his eyes were not satisfied with riches," he was "depriving [him]self of pleasure," and it was all "a grievous task." You don't have to shred your soul to enjoy God's blessings.

A second test of God's blessing is the contentment test. Paul said, "If we have food and covering, with these we shall be content" (1 Timothy 6:8). Now don't misread that. Paul wasn't saying we have to live in a monastery cell on bread and water. He experienced times in his ministry when he could afford a steak dinner (Philippians 4:11–12, discussed later).

But Paul also knew what it was to have just bread and water, or not even that. His point was that once we become discontent with what God provides and "want to get rich" (1 Timothy 6:9), we lose the focus God wants us to have, which is to "pursue righteousness, godliness, faith, love, perseverance and gentleness" (v. 11).

ENJOY THE BLESSINGS GOD HAS FOR YOU

The psalmist's instruction on how to enjoy God's blessings actually begins with a statement concerning the people and the places among whom we will *not* find a true blessing. "How blessed is the man who does not walk in the counsel of the wicked, nor stand in the path of sinners, nor sit in the seat of scoffers!" (Psalm 1:1).

This is not how most people would begin a discussion about what it means to be blessed. Most people would talk about what they do and have, or where they go and who they know. But the psalmist lets us know right off that it is important to know what a blessing looks like and where it can be found. He wants us to be able to spot the difference between the real thing and the world's counterfeit.

I hope you know that not everything people call a blessing is the real thing. Some things that look good in our eyes may prove to be the exact opposite of a blessing. This is a good place to consider several common misconceptions of what it means to be blessed or happy.

Happiness Is Not the Possession of Wealth

Maybe the most common definition of happiness is to equate it with material wealth. Certainly our possessions can be a blessing—if they are gained in a God-honoring way by honest work, we don't destroy our relationship with God and our families to acquire them, and they do not become our god. But you probably know people who have a lot and yet are miserable. The more some people get, the more discontent they are.

There are many problems with this definition of blessing. One is a problem that most people continue to ignore even though thousands of years of human history validate it. Riches alone do not guarantee happiness, peace of mind, security, or any other benefit people seek after. At best, material wealth is a temporary side benefit, although you'd have a hard time convincing most Americans of that.

A second, and even bigger, problem with this view is the dangerous message it sends out. If material things are the measure of blessings, then if you don't have as much as your neighbor or the people on television, by definition you are not as blessed as they are. This means God must not be very happy with you because He sure doesn't seem to be blessing you.

This is a false conclusion, however, that has driven many Christians to frustration as they try to do something Jesus already said is impossible: "You cannot serve God and wealth" (Luke 16:13).

Happiness Is Not Freedom from Pain

Another very popular, but very unbiblical, idea of what it means to be blessed is to be free of any major hassles, problems, and setbacks, including pain or serious illness.

In this definition of blessedness your wife adores you, the roof never leaks, your kids go from being ideal children to responsible and well-behaved teenagers, your mother-in-law is your biggest fan, the job is rolling along, and your worst health problem is a little heartburn. In other words, you may not have it all materially, but at least the sun is shining every day.

Now if you are reading this and saying, "Tony, this only happens on television," I agree. That's why we could call this the "Leave It to Beaver" view of happiness. And it only works in sitcoms.

The Bible's consistent witness is that blessedness has little to do with the absence of trouble or pain in our lives. In fact, many of God's best blessings are hidden inside a painful trial, like the chewy chocolate center of a sucker with a hard outer shell.

James, that in-your-face apostle, wrote: "Consider it all joy, my brethren, when you encounter various trials" (James 1:2). Later, he used the New Testament equivalent of the Hebrew word for "blessed" when he said, "Blessed is a man who perseveres under trial; for once he has been approved, he will receive the crown of life" (v. 12). This is the biblical pattern—and by the way, don't let anyone tell you that only Christians suffer or have hassles either. I don't see anyone offering guarantees of a pain-free life.

Biblical Blessings Allow Us to Enjoy God's Goodness

The Bible is clear that happiness does not depend upon our financial, emotional, or physical circumstances. And yet, God's Word says He wants every one of His children to be blessed. That's why I like the definition of blessedness as the God-given capacity to enjoy His goodness. This definition provides the common denominator that allows any Christian in any age and any circumstance to be a full-fledged candidate for God's blessings.

Paul addressed this in Philippians 4:11–12: "Not that I speak from want, for I have learned to be content in whatever circumstances I am. I know how to get along with humble means, and I also know how to live in prosperity; in any and every circumstance I have learned the secret of being filled and going hungry, both of having abundance and suffering need."

Paul knew how it felt not to be able to pay the bills, and also to have money left at the end of the month. He could sympathize with the worker who is greeted one morning with a layoff notice, and identify with the one who gets a promotion. Paul's secret of contentment, or happiness, was his focus on Christ in "any and every circumstance."

THE BLESSED PERSON
FINDS DELIGHT IN GOD'S WORD

These false views of happiness are typical of the kind of "counsel" or advice that the world offers us, and that Psalm 1:1 counsels us to avoid. We are not to "walk," or conduct our lives, according to the perspective of people who have a man-centered instead of a God-centered worldview.

The "wicked" are not just terribly evil people, but those who do not take God and His Word into account. If you want to enjoy God's goodness, don't go to folk who have no regard for God to get advice on how to live. A lot of us aren't blessed because we're talking to the wrong people.

God's blessings are also not found in "the path of sinners." When the psalmist talks about standing, he means where you hang out and who your "homies" are. The people you stand with are those you identify with and those who have influence over you. The Bible says a person who wants God's blessings will not find them hanging out in the company of people whose primary identity is sinners. These are folk who disregard God's law and make a habit of breaking it.

There is a third place you want to avoid if you are seeking for God's multiplied blessings. The last part of Psalm 1:1 says that the blessed person does not "sit in the seat of scoffers!" A scoffer is someone who makes light of serious things. To scoff is to express contempt or mockery that isn't deserved. The word *seat* suggests someone who sits in judgment. In Old Testament days, the elders of a city sat at the city gate to conduct business, and also to hear cases and render judgments. Thus a scoffer sets himself up as judge and jury in matters he doesn't even understand. And by the way, notice in Psalm 2:4 that God Himself "scoffs" at those who shake their fist in His face. Scoffers are people you don't want to be messing with.

Did you notice the progression in verse 1? The not-so-blessed person, if we can use that term, starts off walking by the wrong crowd and stopping to ask for advice. Then he decides to hang with this crowd, and finally he becomes so comfortable with the wrong people that he's sitting down with them. This is a warning for all of us, because we have all had times when we went from feeling uncomfortable in the wrong situation, to tolerating it, and then, finally, feeling at home with it. If we're not careful this can become a lifestyle, and when that happens we forfeit God's blessings.

You Have to Follow the Right Path to Be Blessed

Now that we know that the path to blessedness is not found in following the world, where can God's blessings be found? The psalmist answered this with a clear declaration that God's blessings are inextricably tied to His Word. "But his delight is in the law of the Lord, and in His law he meditates day and night" (Psalm 1:2).

The word *delight* refers to things or people that bring you pleasure and make you smile just thinking about them. When you delight in someone, you want to be with that person all the time—and when you're not together, you can't stop thinking about that person. When you delight in a song, you play the tune again and again in your mind even when the song isn't playing. In other words, these things are messing with your mind.

That's what it means to delight in something, and the writer of Psalm 1 says that the blessed or happy person delights in God's Word and allows it to occupy his mind. You may say, "I've got a family and a job. I can't sit around all day reading the Bible." That's true, but this is not what the verse is all about. The key is in the word *meditate*.

Meditating on God's Word Brings Blessings

When God talks about the importance of meditating on His Word, don't necessarily assume that to do this you have to sit down in a quiet room trying to focus your mind on Scripture. That's not a bad idea, and most of us do far too little of that. But meditating on the Word can be done wherever you are—just as you can think about a person or an object that brings you great pleasure wherever you are.

To meditate means to chew on the Word, to keep bringing it up and rolling it over in our minds. When you meditate, you are fantasizing over Scripture and what it can do in your life, just as a boy standing out in his backyard with a baseball bat and a ball fantasizes about winning the World Series with a home run and feels the exhilaration of being a hero. Meditation is musing on Scripture until its truth and application to our lives has been clarified by the Holy

Spirit. Anyone who knows how to worry knows how to meditate.

Perhaps the best illustration of meditation is the cow you see in the countryside, slowly chewing and even drooling as she chews her cud. Without getting too graphic in detail, a cow keeps regurgitating a wad of grass and chewing it because a cow has six stomachs to work with, not one. The cow chews that cud until it has finally become palatable to her system, at which point the cud has been thoroughly processed and is ready to go down inside the cow and produce something good, which is the milk we drink.

If we as believers mentally and spiritually processed the Bible as thoroughly as a cow does her cud, there would be a lot of good things coming from our lives. And we can't excuse ourselves by saying we're not very good at this meditation thing. We do it all the time. The problem is that most of us spend most of our time meditating on the wrong things.

For instance, did you know that persistent worry is a negative form of meditation? When you are worried about something, you can't get it out of your mind no matter what you are doing. A lot of people spend a lot of time "meditating" on their financial situation. Some people meditate on their favorite television program or sports team. How do I know that? Because what we meditate on, what we think about the most and what consumes our affections, comes out in what we talk about the most.

So let's not use the "I don't know how to meditate" excuse as a reason for not focusing our minds on God and His Word. I will grant you that letting God's Word get such a grip on you that you can't stop thinking about it takes a little work at first, especially if this is a new concept to you. The first time we hear or read the Word, it may not connect. But instead of just putting it out of our minds and going on, we need to work that thing like a cow working her cud. We need to think about how our lives would look if we systematically and seriously applied the Scripture we are dealing with.

Too often, though, we settle for a Bible verse a day to keep the devil away, because somehow we have the idea that the Word is too hard to understand. Or we're content just to hear someone else talk about it.

Unfortunately, many Christians are spiritual bulimics. A bulimic is a person with a craving for food who does not want to be affected by that food. So a bulimic will eat and then go to the bathroom and throw up so the food doesn't have time to have any effect. Many Christians go to church on Sunday or Wednesday to enjoy a good meal from God's Word, but they go out the doors and toss that food out of their spiritual systems—with the result that they begin to waste away from lack of nourishment.

One way to avoid this syndrome is to meditate on the Word—to roll it over and over in your mind and ask, "God, how does Your Word affect what I'm facing right now? What does it say about my response to what I'm facing? How can Your Word change what I'm thinking and feeling right now if my attitude is not right? How does Your Word equip me to deal with the things I am facing?"

Meditation connects God's Word to life's realities. The difference between hearing God's Word and being blessed by it is called meditation.

Why does God want us to meditate on His Word? There are many reasons, including the need to avoid sin (see Psalm 119:11). The subject of this chapter suggests another reason. The Bible is the repository of our spiritual blessings. It is the means by which we bring heaven down to earth, which is a good description of what it means to be blessed.

I love the story of the little boy who had just taken his first ride in an elevator and was trying to explain it. "I went into this little room," he said excitedly, "and the upstairs came down!" Blessing is when heaven comes down and the glory of God fills your soul. He gives you the capacity to enjoy Him and His goodness, regardless of what is happening around you.

WE ARE BLESSED TO FIND OUR DELIGHT IN GOD'S WORD

We've seen how to avoid places where God's blessing is not found, and where to locate it. Now let's consider what the blessing of God does for the person who knows how to enjoy it. Psalm 1:3

says of the blessed person, "He will be like a tree firmly planted by streams of water, which yields its fruit in its season and its leaf does not wither; and in whatever he does, he prospers."

You Will Be Well Rooted

A tree is a great word picture of someone who is enjoying God's goodness and blessings in spite of circumstances. The Bible uses grass to illustrate something that is transitory (see Isaiah 40:7–8 and Matthew 6:30). But a tree illustrates that which is meant to last. You cut down grass when it begins to grow too long, but you don't mow down a tree. Grass is tied down tight to the ground, but a tree soars above it.

You Will Be Firmly Established

The psalmist continued to describe the blessed person as a tree "firmly planted." This is a picture of stability, being firmly anchored. I can get a very tall ladder, lean it against a building, then climb to the top of the ladder and stand there. But there is a fundamental, all-important difference between me on a ladder and a tree. Unless Superman is holding that ladder for me, I am not firmly planted. The next puff of wind could blow me over. In fact, I am not about to climb to the top of a tall ladder and stand there just to demonstrate the truth of this illustration!

When you are firmly planted, the stuff that used to blow you over doesn't knock you down anymore. You may bend in the wind, but your root system will hold you if your roots are planted deeply in God's Word. The writer of Hebrews called our hope in Christ "an anchor of the soul" (6:19). Guess where we learn about that hope? In God's revealed Word.

You Will Be Well Nourished

The blessing of God doesn't just leave you planted in the middle of a desert, either. Instead, you are planted "by streams of water," an Old Testament phrase for irrigation ditches. If you have ever been to Israel, you know that irrigation has been the key to making the desert over there blossom like a rose.

The beauty of an irrigation system is that it carries water to the tree regardless of the external circumstances. The important thing is not what is happening on the surface, but underground where the water runs deep and the tree can drink.

This brings us back to the definition of a blessing as the capacity to enjoy God's goodness. Being blessed doesn't mean the weather is nice all the time or the rain always comes just when it is needed. Being blessed means the internal is fine even if the external is falling apart. Being blessed means that you can drink of God's goodness even when conditions are dry because your roots are attached to the ever-flowing spring of His eternal Word. The person who knows and lives in God's Word enjoys a continuous source of life.

You Will Be Fruitful

The middle of Psalm 1:3 says further that a blessed person will "yield" or produce fruit. This refers to being productive, taking that internal nourishment and refreshment and turning it into something that other people around you can enjoy, too. Someone has said that Christians are blessed to be a blessing. That's a good way to put it. If you're being blessed but all you are passing on to others is a sour, dried-up piece of fruit, your blessing is stopping at the wrong station. Fruit always reflects the character of the tree it comes from.

Your capacity to enjoy God should give you something to share. A tree doesn't yield fruit for its own consumption. This is the problem with so much of today's teaching on how to get God's blessings. It tends to turn Christians into self-focused, "gimme, gimme" people. The emphasis is on how I can get my goodies from God, never mind you.

But fruit always exists for the benefit of another. So one way you know you're blessed is that you are being a blessing. Other folks can take a bite out of you and be blessed. When fruit starts eating itself, that means disease has set in and corrective action is required.

Notice also that the leaf of the blessed person "does not wither." This tree is an evergreen, in other words. There is a freshness and vibrancy about a person who is being blessed of God. It doesn't mean we never get down or feel negative. The Bible doesn't say the leaves won't shake in the wind sometimes. Those are the external circumstances we can't control. But the leaves of our lives won't die and fall off from the internal lack of water when we are tapped into God and His Word.

You Will Prosper

Now look at the summary statement of this great passage. Whatever the blessed person does "prospers." Whatever this person touches comes back to life if it was dead. God can make such a great promise because the person who is delighting in and meditating on His Word will reflect God's mind and heart in what he or she desires and does. God's blessing will prosper you in that you will know His smile of pleasure on your life.

That's quite a package of blessing. Do you want to be blessed? I believe you do, and so do I. There is no question about God's desire to deliver His blessings. The only question is whether we are putting ourselves in a position to receive His goodness. To be blessed, you need to go deep with God and His Word.

Have you ever thought about the fact that fish don't get upset when it rains—or even when there is a "perfect storm" at sea with hundred-foot waves? The reason fish don't get upset and all stressed out when a storm hits is that they can go deeper than the storm. I'm told that a storm can only penetrate about the first twenty-five feet of ocean depth—so when a storm hits, fish just go deeper than the storm can reach.

So if there is turbulence in your world, just go deeper. If there's struggle in your life, just go deeper. Let God's Word take you deeper than you have ever gone before. Meditate on it. Think about it; let it penetrate the folds of your mind and hit your heart. Let God take you deep into His Word, and you'll find the place of true blessing.

14

THE BIBLE BRINGS SPIRITUAL FREEDOM

When American and coalition forces struck against Saddam Hussein's regime in Iraq in March 2003, the military effort was known as Operation Iraqi Freedom. By May, Hussein had been driven from power and forced into hiding prior to his capture.

But toppling Saddam and his brutal dictatorship was just one of the objectives that had to be achieved to secure freedom for the people of Iraq. The problem was that even though the enemy was defeated, many of its members and sympathizers were still around and ready to cause havoc. If America and her allies had simply quit and gone home when the oppressive Iraqi regime was defeated, the freedom of the Iraqi people from their old taskmaster would have been short-lived. So the campaign in Iraq became Operation Enduring Freedom to secure the freedom that had been established. The coalition did not pay such a high price just to see the people they had liberated fall back under the domination of the enemy.

In other words, Iraq was free, but her people needed to be "free indeed," to use a phrase Jesus used in a key passage from God's transforming Word. Freedom is a prize that people have treasured, fought for, and guarded throughout history, a struggle necessitated by the fact that oppression by one person or group over another is as old as the human race. The people of Israel in Jesus' day longed for freedom from the Roman armies who had invaded the land of Israel, conquered it, and made it a part of their kingdom.

Jesus knew that Israel was chafing under the rule of Rome, and that many Jews were looking for a liberator who would drive out the Romans and set them free. Jesus was intensely interested in the subject of freedom, and He was well aware that some of His followers and others who had seen His power and miracles were hoping that He was the Messiah/Conqueror they wanted. But Jesus had come to bestow a totally different kind of liberty on people who were in bondage to Satan, the true oppressor, whose tool of oppression and tyranny is sin.

Not everyone Jesus met wanted that kind of freedom, or even felt they needed it. So it's not surprising that Jesus' view clashed with the people's view one day when the Lord raised the issue of true freedom. In the course of this discussion we learn that the truth of God's Word is the source of the spiritual freedom we enjoy.

JESUS TAUGHT THE
TRUTH THAT SETS US FREE

The apostle John records that as Jesus spoke to a crowd of Jews that day, He told some people who believed in Him, "If you continue in My word, then you are truly disciples of Mine; and you will know the truth, and the truth will make you free" (John 8:31–32). This provoked angry reaction from the crowd, particularly the idea that Jesus' hearers did not really know what it meant to be free.

Whenever you tell people they need to be free, an assumption is being made that they are in slavery of some kind. The only people who need to be set free are those who are enslaved to someone or something, or under tyranny, and need to be liberated. It's bad enough to be a slave, but it's even worse to be ignorant of your slavery. Jesus was talking to people who didn't realize they were slaves and so did not recognize their need for Jesus' offer of freedom. They did not realize how bad their slavery really was.

Spiritual Freedom Is a Special Kind of Freedom

Let's define the concept of freedom from a biblical standpoint. To be spiritually free is to be liberated from slavery to sin in order to become all that we were meant to be. Notice that this definition says nothing about being able to do whatever you want whenever you want, without any restraints or restrictions at all. This is often the world's idea of freedom, but people who live like this are actually in the worst slavery of all, which is slavery to their own sinful desires. Freedom in the Bible has nothing to do with the removal of all boundaries or limitations, but with the ability to be and to do what God wants within His boundaries.

We see the nature of true freedom illustrated all around us. A fish is free to roam around the ocean, but a fish that decides he is tired of living within the boundary of water and wants to live on dry land will not be free, just dead. You may be free to swing your fist around all you want, but your freedom ends where my nose begins! Freedom is not the absence of boundaries, but right living within those boundaries.

Many people also have the mistaken idea that freedom means having no master, no one who can tell them what to do. But true freedom is having the right master, one who knows how to help you reach your potential and not limit you to less than you were created to be. The importance of having the right master was the crux of the message that Jesus delivered to the crowd that stood around Him in John 8 as He taught them about the real nature of spiritual slavery and freedom.

Jesus' implication that His hearers were not yet free brought this angry reaction: "We are Abraham's descendants and have never yet been enslaved to anyone; how is it that You say, 'You will become free'?" (v. 33). That was quite a statement coming from people whose nation had endured a long history of bondage. These Jews said they had never been anybody's slaves, but their ancestors were in bondage in Egypt for four hundred years. Later generations had been conquered and carried off into captivity by the Assyrians and Babylonians, and then they came under the rule of Persia.

In fact, the people who were with Jesus that day were under the domination of Rome. They may not have been in chains, but the Israelites of Jesus' day were a subjugated people. They had been in bondage so long they forgot what it was like to be free. You can get used to being a slave. It can become such a habit that you don't even remember that there is something called freedom.

Sin Is the Cause of Spiritual Slavery

The kind of slavery Jesus had in mind had nothing to do with political boundaries or human kingdoms. He answered the boast of the people that they had never been slaves with a description of true slavery: "Truly, truly, I say to you, everyone who commits sin is the slave of sin. The slave does not remain in the house forever; the son does remain forever" (John 8:34–35). Here Jesus clearly identified sin as the cause of slavery.

This is true even in the natural realm, because all human slavery is the result of the sinful domination of one people by another. And in the spiritual realm, all bondage can either directly or indirectly be traced back to the presence of sin. Slavery comes because people reject God and rebel against Him and His plan of salvation.

This is the type of slavery Jesus meant when He told the Jews that whoever commits sin is the slave of sin. That indictment covers every person who has ever been born, regardless of our pedigree or status in the world. And while slavery in the human realm does not always lead to death, every person who commits sin and fails to find God's remedy is headed toward eternal death, because "the wages of sin is death" (Romans 6:23). So while the Jews wanted

Jesus to liberate them from Rome, He wanted to set them free from certain spiritual death to enjoy all the fullness and blessings of the spiritual life He would purchase on the cross.

God's Truth Applies to Our Lives Today

How does this freedom apply to us today? If you are not spiritually free, it is either because you have never embraced the truth of the gospel and come to Jesus for salvation, or because as a Christian you are not continuing in the truth. Remember Jesus said, "If you continue in My word, then you are truly disciples of Mine" (John 8:31). We'll get into this issue later.

Notice also where true freedom is located. Jesus said freedom is found in knowing "the truth" (v. 32), which is another way of describing His Word, the Bible. Don't miss the fact that just having a Bible in your house or under your arm at church is not enough to bring freedom. You must *know* the truth. You must allow the Word of God to unlock your mind and fill it with the knowledge of God that brings salvation.

There is a correlation between the process of knowing spiritual truth and the process of getting an education. We encourage and challenge our children to get the best education they possibly can because gaining knowledge helps them unlock and maximize their potential, and then it opens doors of opportunity for them.

Now if knowledge can do this in the natural realm, imagine what God's truth can do in the supernatural realm. It opens doors you couldn't normally get through. It allows you to become truly free. Growth in spiritual truth brings growth in spiritual freedom, which is freedom from sin to become all that you were created and redeemed to be.

Jesus spoke of *the* truth in John 8:32. The definite article makes all the difference, because we are talking about a definitive body of truth, not a bunch of competing "truths" or ideologies. There is no such thing as your truth and my truth. There is only the truth. Jesus said in John 17:17, "Your word is truth." God's Word is the final word on every subject. It doesn't matter whether people feel enslaved or not. Jesus said that everyone who commits sin is a slave to sin.

God's True Children Know His Truth

This was the problem with the people Jesus was talking to in John 8:31–36. Their argument was that that they were Abraham's children (see also v. 39) and therefore free, not slaves of anyone. So Jesus drew on the case of old Abe and his offspring to make His point.

Abraham had two sons, Ishmael and Isaac. Ishmael was born of the slave Hagar and was sent out of Abraham's house because he was not the son of promise, who was Isaac. Isaac got to stay in his father's house because he was the legitimate son. Ishmael was treated like a slave, but Isaac was treated like a true son. A slave only comes into the master's house when he is invited or has permission. A son comes into the house anytime he wants because it is his home, and he gets to enjoy the benefits and privileges of being his father's heir.

The Jews saw themselves as the true sons and Jesus as the illegitimate son (see v. 41), but Jesus moved the conversation into a whole new realm when He told them they were slaves of sin. In fact, He did not even wait for them to answer or make another protest, but He hit them with the ringer by saying, "So if the Son makes you free, you will be free indeed" (v. 36).

Jesus was saying that He is the legitimate Son of God who has access to His Father's house forever. Therefore, He alone has the power to set people free from sin. Anyone else who claims to do this is an imposter, a slave trying to masquerade as the Son. But all imposters who try to infringe on the Son's authority will get booted out of the house. They may look legitimate for now and wield some power, but they will eventually be tossed out because in God's house, Jesus Christ is the Son—and as such, He holds all the keys to freedom.

So it was clear to everyone who was present that day that Jesus was talking about the Son of God, and claiming that title for Himself. His point was unmistakable. They were not sons of God but sinners in bondage to their sin, and the true Son was the only one who could set them "free indeed" (John 8:36).

TRUE FREEDOM MEANS
ABIDING IN GOD'S WORD

Now we get into the good stuff, which is the importance of abiding in God's Word. This is where the Bible's transforming power is unleashed and we are set free to become all that God saved us to be.

Let's double back to John 8:31 and abide there for a while, because it is easy to read over what Jesus said and focus on the controversy that followed. He said that His true followers are those who "continue" in His Word. This is the Greek verb that means "to abide, to stay, to remain." Jesus used this same verb again in John 15:7, a great promise for abiders: "If you abide in Me, and My words abide in you, ask whatever you wish, and it will be done for you."

God Wants His Word to Be Fully at Home Within Us

There are basically two ways you can abide or stay. You can stay because you *have to*, as when a father says to his teenager, "You're grounded for two weeks! You aren't going anywhere but to school and straight home!" Or, you can stay because you *want to*, like your daughter's boyfriend who thinks he's part of the family and wants to hang out at your house all the time.

This second picture is what Jesus meant by abiding. It means to feel completely at home, to be comfortable with, to hang out with because there's no place you'd rather be and no one you'd rather be with.

Anybody who has been in love knows how to abide. Think about when you first fell in love. You called your beloved when there was no reason to call, and you stayed on the phone when neither one of you had anything of importance left to say. And as soon as you hung up, you wished you had stayed on the line and you began thinking about the next call or that glorious moment when you would be together again.

This is a convicting question, but I need to ask it: Does this describe your passion for God's Word and the anticipation of meeting with Him in the pages of the Bible? If not, you're not really abiding in His Word—and the consequences of failing to abide are devastating.

Someone may say, "This sounds a little radical to me. Is it really essential that I become so intense about the Bible?"

Short answer: Yes, it is! It is absolutely essential that you let God's Word be at home in you. There are several reasons for this. The first and most important is that this is God's revealed will for you. We just read it in John 8:31 and 15:7. Abiding in the Word is not for super saints. It is what God expects from each of His children.

A second reason you need to abide has to do with our redeemed, but still sin-affected, human nature. Embracing truth does not come naturally to us. We have to work at learning and living it because we were "by nature children of wrath" (Ephesians 2:3), whose minds were in total rebellion against God.

We are new creations now in Christ, but we are still carrying the scars of sin—which you realize when you try to do the right thing and wind up doing the wrong thing. As the bumper sticker says, "Christians aren't perfect, just forgiven." At least we're in good company, because in Romans 6–7 the apostle Paul wrestled with the question, "If I'm a Christian, why am I doing the very things I don't want to do?" His answer was that it was "the law of sin which is in my members [of his body]" (Romans 7:23).

But keep on reading, because Paul wasn't making excuses for himself or for us. Here is his conclusion to the matter: "Thanks be to God through Jesus Christ our Lord!" (v. 25). Why? Because "the law of the Spirit of life in Christ Jesus *has set [me] free* from the law of sin and death" (Romans 8:2, italics added).

We Can't Let Anyone Enslave Us Again

This is the Christian's "emancipation proclamation." But Paul also told the Galatians, "It was for freedom that Christ set us free;

therefore keep standing firm and do not be subject again to a yoke of slavery" (5:1). How can someone who has been set free by Jesus Christ be in danger of becoming a slave again?

We can rule out the loss of salvation, because that can never happen to true believers. Salvation was not the issue in Galatians 5, but whether these Christians would allow themselves to be subjected to the demands of the Mosaic Law instead of living by grace. One of the ironies of the Christian life is that the Bible tells us to be what we are. God says we need to behave like His children because that's what we are. And we are told to make sure we live in the freedom that Christ purchased for us because we are, in fact, free people.

Now let's make an important connection that links God's Word and spiritual freedom with our need to abide in the Word until we're completely at home in it and it's at home in us. We know that Jesus said it is *knowing* the truth that sets us free. That statement has great relevance to the problem Paul was wrestling with at Galatia.

The Galatians were in danger of being brought under bondage by a group called the Judaizers, who ran around following Paul into each city where he preached and tried to make Gentile Christians put themselves under the Jewish law. So the issue was the very nature of God's salvation. Was Paul right in preaching grace totally apart from law, or were the Judaizers correct that Gentiles had to become like Jews to be saved?

I don't think I even have to answer that for you. The Galatians had heard the truth from Paul and knew that salvation was by grace alone through faith. So why were they falling for the Judaizers' line? They were being hoodwinked because they had forgotten the truth Paul taught them. In other words, they weren't abiding in the truth, which allowed these false teachers to pull a fast one on them by poisoning the "pot" of God's truth with error, just as one of the prophets of Elijah's day poisoned a pot of good stew with "wild gourds" (2 Kings 4:38–41; see the conclusion for a discussion of this passage). That's why Paul asked with great anguish, "You foolish Galatians, who has bewitched you?" (Galatians 3:1). He was saying, "I gave you the truth. How could you possibly let anybody talk you out of it?"

This is the question that we ought to be asking ourselves today, because the cults are going up and down our streets talking thousands of people who were raised in church out of whatever it is they believe and into those cults.

Now let me bring this home and talk about our freedom. If it is possible to be Christians and yet not live in the freedom Christ gave us, it can only mean that something has us in bondage that ought not to have control over us. This could be almost any sin or weakness to which our human flesh is susceptible: bitterness, unforgiveness, lack of self-control in an area such as food, greed, a critical spirit, or an addiction to drugs, alcohol, sex, or some other bodily appetite. We could even be in bondage because we allowed somebody to wrap us up so tightly in religious legalism that we're more concerned about obeying a list of rules than we are about pleasing Christ.

The antidote to bondage for the Christian is abiding in the Word. It's pretty hard for the devil or anyone else to put one over on you when God's Word is so integral a part of your being that you automatically think and react biblically. But that kind of discipline only comes from hanging out in the Word until you start to absorb it through every pore in your body.

We Don't Want to Abide in God's Word

This is the real problem, isn't it? I know I am writing to someone who paces back and forth in front of the microwave waiting for a two-minute meal to finish. Have you ever done that? Tell the truth and shame the devil.

Abiding doesn't mesh very well with our instant world. But the problem with just zapping food in the microwave is that it can be all hot and steamy and seem well-cooked, but when you bite into it the center is still crunchy and frozen. If you want a well-cooked chicken, that bird has to "abide" in the oven or the Crock-Pot until the meat is separated from the bone.

The lack of desire or commitment to abide in the Word helps

to explain a question that a lot of Christians have. When they look around, it seems that everybody is growing and enjoying victory but them. So they conclude that God must relate to other believers better than He relates to them. They figure other Christians have an inside track to God that they don't have. But that's not the case at all.

The answer can be found in an incident recorded in John 2:23–25. The Bible says that many people believed in Jesus when they saw His miracles. "But Jesus, on His part, was not entrusting Himself to them, for He knew all men, and because He did not need anyone to testify concerning man, for He Himself knew what was in man" (vv. 24–25).

Someone may read that and say, "See, it's true. Jesus doesn't relate to all believers equally. He kept these people at arm's length even though they believed in Him." But the issue here is why He did that. Based on His perfect knowledge of the human heart, and the fact that many of His early disciples later deserted Him when things got tough (see John 6:64, 66), Jesus knew who was real and who wasn't. He doesn't play favorites; it's just that He is not going to commit Himself to someone who only wants a casual relationship.

What I'm saying is that this business of abiding in Christ and letting His Word abide in us is serious stuff. That leads to another important question we need to discuss.

HOW CAN WE KNOW
WE ARE ABIDING IN THE WORD?

We are abiding in Christ, and His Word is abiding in us, when we are enjoying His company through the Word. Now it goes without saying that this means more than just reading the Bible occasionally. It's reading the Bible in order to snuggle up close to God and spend unhurried time in His presence. To get an idea of what abiding looks like, picture a person running to his or her favorite spot and settling in with a newly arrived love letter to read.

Read the Bible As God's Love Letter to You

I'm sure you've heard it said that we should read the Bible the way we would read a love letter. I know you didn't just read a "verse" or two of love letters and then lay them aside for a few days until you had a free minute or there was nothing good on television. You devoured each letter, weighing the nuances and deeper meanings of every word because the relationship behind those letters was more important to you than your food or other comforts. If you're a guy, you probably sniffed your love letters over and over again. In fact, you may still have them somewhere.

When the Bible becomes that precious to us, then we will begin to experience what Jesus meant when He said, "If the Son makes you free, you will be free indeed" (John 8:36). "Indeed" means "sho 'nuff," or certainly. It means this is the real deal, because the Son has the authority to set us free and keep us free. It means to look for Jesus, because when He shows up, you know everything is going to be OK.

I remember once in college when I returned to campus on the weekend after being away. If you ever lived in a college dorm, you know how deserted those places can be on the weekend. Well, not only was my dorm empty, but as I walked across campus I didn't see anyone, either. I started feeling a little creepy because before I left for the weekend, we had just studied the rapture of the church and how Jesus was coming back for the saints. So I began to wonder if the Rapture had occurred and I had been left behind because nobody was in sight.

Then out of nowhere came Marvin, but his presence didn't bring me any comfort at all. That's because Marvin was a prankster and troublemaker, one of those guys who was always trying to stir something up. I saw Marvin and thought to myself, "That doesn't mean anything. Marvin would have been left behind anyway!"

Seeing Marvin did not free me from my fears. But when Jesus is on the scene, all fear is gone.

Don't Rush Your Time in God's Holy Presence

I remember talking once with a greatly respected Christian author and speaker who is well known for his deep, intimate relationship with God. I asked him for his secret, and he said, "Well, if there is a secret it boils down to one phrase: unhurried time in God's presence."

As I thought about it, I was struck by the wisdom of what he said. Most of our time with God is hurried time. We treat Him and His Word like we treat the food in the microwave, tapping our fingers and looking at our watches to see how long it's going to take to get something good from Him that will feed us until we get hungry again.

But God does not operate on the clock, let alone a two-minute timer. Try setting a timer and then saying to your wife, "I'll give you two minutes of my abiding, and then I'm gone." The man I was talking to said he typically gets up at four in the morning to spend two or three hours reading the Bible, worshiping, praying, thinking, and just being in God's presence without hurrying. And here's the interesting thing. He told me that doing this will solve problems for him during the day that he would have had to solve himself, except that he just tries to put God so far out front that by the time he arrives there, God has already addressed the need.

Now I'm not saying this man's way is the only way. But I hope you are really hearing his point. Most of us would say, "Wow! I can't spend three hours a day in prayer and worship. I've got stuff to do. What does God expect of me, anyway?"

Well, Jesus died for us, so He expects everything we have. But what He really wants is for you to spend as much time with Him as you want to spend. And the more time in His presence, the more problems get solved before you even get there. Don't ever believe that time spent with God means less time for "productive" activities.

God didn't just set you free on Calvary so you could avoid hell. He wants to set you "free indeed" to enjoy a life in His presence. He gave you His Word so you can abide in it until His truth oozes from every pore of your being and changes you from the inside out.

THE BIBLE GIVES SPIRITUAL VICTORY

Ⓐ book by former basketball great Kareem Abdul-Jabbar tells the story of the 761st tank battalion, an African-American unit that performed valiantly in Europe during World War II. Wartime prejudice against black soldiers kept these troops out of the battle for almost two years, but once they were allowed to fight, they did so bravely and won many medals for valor.

Unlike most soldiers, however, the heroes of the 761st had another battle to face once victory in Europe was achieved. These men had to come home to a society that relegated them to second-class citizenship and fight the second half of what was often called the "double V" campaign (based on Winston Churchill's famous "V for Victory" sign): victory over the Nazis in Europe and victory over racism at home.

It's a tragedy to make people fight a battle that shouldn't have to be fought at all, especially when it drains their time and energies that are needed elsewhere. This is exactly the strategy that our enemy the devil uses when he comes at us in spiritual warfare. He tries to discourage and distract us from the real battle and convince us that we have to fight him on his terms, not God's, and in the power of our own flesh, not in the strength that God provides. Tragically, Satan succeeds in this strategy far too often, the proof of which is the number of defeated Christians who are wondering what hit them.

But God's Word has an announcement for the devil. In the words of David to Goliath, "The battle is the Lord's and He will give you into our hands" (1 Samuel 17:47). The enemy Goliath, who stood for all that was evil, was a terrifying presence with his huge size, heavy armor, and gigantic weapons. But like our enemy Satan (see 1 Peter 5:8), Goliath was a toothless lion despite his roaring because David was fighting in the Lord's name and strength. In the end, it was no contest. David's little stones and slings were the mighty weapons, not Goliath's huge spear, because this was not really a battle of the flesh but of the spirit.

The psalmist proclaimed, "O sing to the Lord a new song, for He has done wonderful things, His right hand and His holy arm have gained the victory for Him" (Psalm 98:1). This is the victory we want as Christians, what the apostle John called "the victory that has overcome the world—our faith" (1 John 5:4).

Now if we are talking about achieving victory and the context of that victory is warfare, then we need the right weapons to fight with. This is where the Bible comes in, for it not only tells us about the weapons God has given us, but it *is* our primary weapon for defeating Satan and laying claim to spiritual victory.

THE BIBLE IS OUR PRIMARY
WEAPON FOR SPIRITUAL WARFARE

If you're tracking with me, you may already be thinking of Ephesians 6, in which Paul explained the nature of our battle and the armament God wants us to use. The specific pieces of the Christian's armor are described in verses 14–17a, which you can review for yourself. I want to focus on the one offensive weapon available to us in this battle, "the sword of the Spirit, which is the word of God" (v. 17b).

Our Battle Is Spiritual, not Physical

Now the reason this is the Spirit's sword instead of a steel blade is that "our struggle is not against flesh and blood, but against the rulers, against the powers, against the world forces of this darkness, against the spiritual forces of wickedness in the heavenly places" (Ephesians 6:12; see also 2 Corinthians 10:3–4). If you're fighting with other people because you think they are the enemies keeping you from enjoying the victory God promises to His people, you are on the wrong battlefield. Our real battle is in the spiritual realm against Satan and his array of demons, who can use people to harass and wound us.

If you have ever read any of my books, you know that one of the overarching principles that I believe governs the universe is that what happens in the earthly realm is simply a reflection of and a reaction to what happens in the spiritual realm. The spiritual always governs the physical.

"Heavenly places" is the realm where our battle as Christians is located. But guess what else? It is also the realm where our spiritual blessings are located (see Ephesians 1:3). So if you want to get to God's blessings and there is an army arrayed up against you whose goal is to keep you from those blessings and mess up your life to boot, then you had better know how to do battle with the enemy in that realm. This is why Paul did not want us either to dismiss or to overlook the spiritual realm and what is going on there.

Our Victory Is Already Assured

Ephesians 6 makes it crystal clear that when it comes to spiritual warfare and the issue of our victory, the matter has already been settled. How do we know? Well, if you read the spiritual warfare passage in Ephesians 6:10–17, you will notice that nowhere are we told to attack the enemy and try to overcome him. Instead, our job is to "stand firm" (v. 11; see also vv. 13–14).

Now why would a soldier be told to stand firm instead of attack and advance? Because he already has the territory his commander wants to take, and his job is to hold on to it. Jesus Christ defeated the devil and all of his army on the cross, and nothing can cancel out that victory. The result is that we are not fighting for victory, but from a position of victory. Satan is a defeated foe.

I know the next question someone usually asks. "Well, if Satan is whipped already, why is he pounding away on me? He doesn't feel like a defeated enemy the way he's attacking me."

Every Christian has felt this way at one time or another. It reminds me of the boxer who was getting pounded by his opponent. After every round, when he would come back to his corner bruised and bleeding, his manager would rub his shoulders and tell him enthusiastically, "You're doing great, kid. He hasn't laid a glove on you!" Each time his manager said this, the boxer would look at him funny out of his one eye that wasn't swollen shut, shrug, and head back out for another pounding.

This went on for about eight rounds—and sure enough, once more when the boxer sat down in his corner, his manager whispered in his ear, "Hang in there. He hasn't laid a glove on you yet."

The exasperated boxer couldn't take it anymore and yelled out, "Then somebody better be watching that referee!"

That's how it is for us at times. But God wants us to know that the outcome of this battle has been determined, even if we get an occasional black eye or a blow to the stomach. We still have to fight a battle whose outcome is certain, and we are told to hold on to the victory that is already ours—which is yet another irony of the Christian life. But we must understand that we are the victors, or otherwise we won't have the right mind-set for the battle.

Satan may be able to sting you once in a while, but he's firing a BB gun and not a lethal weapon. Knowing this ought to turn our fear into courage, because once you realize your enemy has a popgun instead of a Howitzer, it dawns on you that you have nothing to be afraid of. And you can turn around, face the enemy, and stand firm.

God Tells Us How to Wield the Sword of His Word

We said earlier that "the sword of the Spirit," the "word of God," is the only offensive weapon in our Christian armory. Paul likened it to a particular kind of sword that Roman soldiers carried, and that all of his readers in Ephesus would be very familiar with.

The sword mentioned in Ephesians 6:17 is not the long sword we usually see in the old movies hung at a soldier's side in a sheath. The word for "sword" here refers to a much shorter, daggerlike weapon that a soldier carried in his belt for quick access in case he got into closer combat and needed a precision weapon to strike a decisive blow. A soldier sometimes used both hands to wield his long sword, flailing and slashing away at the enemy. But his short, dagger-like sword could be applied much more directly and with deadly result.

This was the same kind of sword that Peter used in the Garden of Gethsemane to cut off a man's ear when Jesus was being arrested (see John 18:10). This may explain why Peter was able to grab it and strike before anyone could stop him. If Peter had reached across his body to draw out a long sword from its sheath, the others might have had time to react.

But it was done in a flash, and I think Peter accomplished his intent. We are often told that Peter really meant to take the guy's head off, but swung wildly and only got his ear. I don't think so, because that's not the way this sword was handled. Think precision cut here, more like a doctor with a scalpel than a man flailing wildly with a big sword.

I'm making this point in depth because this is the word that Paul chose under the Holy Spirit's inspiration to describe what God's Word is designed to do for us in spiritual battle. It's important to understand that spiritual warfare is not swinging at the enemy from a distance, but close-in combat. The devil may be beaten, but he is still alive and well for now, and he loves nothing better than to get all up in your face and kick sand in it. That's why victory in spiritual warfare requires a weapon that can deliver precision blows.

We Must Have God's Word Ready at Hand

Another Greek word in Ephesians 6:17 is very enlightening as we seek to understand how to win at spiritual warfare. Paul called the Spirit's dagger "the word of God"—but we need to stop here, because this is not the ordinary word for Scripture. Paul did not use the familiar Greek word *logos*, which looks at the Bible in its entirety as the received body of God's truth.

Instead, Paul used the word *rhema,* which means "an utterance," and looks at the Bible not as a bound volume of sixty-six books, but as a weapon ready at hand to be used in a definite way at a definite time of need.

This is where it gets exciting! Paul was saying that if we want to be victorious in spiritual warfare, we must be able to draw on specific truths from the Bible in specific situations to counter specific temptations and attacks from the Enemy.

There are many ways to illustrate this. For instance, there are children's books available that use cute stories, and maybe a little song or poem, to teach young children not to be afraid of the dark. When you sit down and read that book to your child to help him know there is no reason to be afraid of the dark, you are giving him or her the *logos,* a body of content that is true.

But when that child wakes up scared in the middle of the night and is able to remember that little poem, or sing that song, to overcome fear and go back to sleep instead of screaming in terror for you, he or she has just used a *rhema* from that *logos* to meet a specific need in a specific situation.

I like to use sports analogies, so when I think of the difference between *logos* and *rhema* I picture a tennis racket or a golf club. A tennis racket hanging in the garage has built into it all the qualities needed to be victorious, but there is a world of difference between hanging a racket in the garage and putting it in the hands of Venus or Serena Williams. They can use that racket with surgeonlike precision to slice up their opponents and win tournaments.

The same is true of a set of golf clubs. They may look great standing in the corner of your den or office. You may have paid a lot of money for them, and you love to show them to people. Those clubs won't do much in your den, however. But give them to Tiger Woods, and we're talking a potential Grand Slam sweep because he can use those clubs to drop a shot within inches of a little cup from a hundred and fifty yards away.

GOD'S WORD IS POWERFUL IN BATTLE

I hope you see where I'm going. You can have the entire *logos* of God on your shelf, the very Word of God that is complete and true in every syllable, and yet not be well-armed for spiritual warfare because you don't know how to draw on the *rhema* of God when you are under attack. You can own a Bible factory and yet be basically defenseless against Satan if you are not well practiced in handling the Word of truth.

Until the *logos* of God—that Bible under your arm at church—also becomes the *rhema* in your hand to defeat the Enemy, you won't see the Bible's power at work. As long as the Bible is just a bunch of general statements to you, you'll be a general Christian knowing general truth, and you'll get general results. But a believer who is filled and controlled by the Holy Spirit, and who knows how to handle the sword of the Spirit in specific spiritual encounters, can win any battle in any realm.

THE BIBLE IS POWERFUL—REGARDLESS

Now don't misunderstand. We're not saying that the Bible only becomes sharp and powerful when we start using it properly. In fact, one of the foundational verses of this entire study says exactly the opposite. "The word [*logos*] of God is living and active and sharper than any two-edged sword" (Hebrews 4:12). Guess what word for "sword" the writer used here? You got it—the Roman short sword/dagger we've been talking about. So here is a text that joins the logos with this concept of a sharp, precision weapon, just as Ephesians 6:17 does with the *rhema*. God's Word is sharp regardless of whether we ever discover that reality for ourselves.

The reason you want to learn the Bible generally is so that you can use it specifically when the need arises for victory in spiritual warfare. I want to be victorious in my Christian life, not just barely hang on until I die or Jesus returns with angelic reinforcements. The great thing about the *rhema* of the Spirit is that it can keep you out of unnecessary battles so you can save your energies for the real warfare.

I love the story of the little boy whose mother had made two fresh pies and put them in the pantry to cool with strict orders not to touch them because they were for guests at dinner that evening. A while later, mama realized it was far too quiet and called out, "Johnny, where are you?"

"In the pantry," came a quivering little voice.

"What are you doing in the pantry?"

"Trying to resist temptation!"

This is exactly what so many Christians do. If you like doughnuts but don't need them, I highly suggest that you not visit the doughnut shop each week to see how few doughnuts you can eat. Instead, stick a *rhema* in your belt by memorizing 1 Corinthians 6:12, "All things are lawful for me, but I will not be mastered by anything" and 9:27, "I discipline my body and make it my slave, so that, after I have preached to others, I myself will not be disqualified." Then ask the Holy Spirit to bring those verses to mind when you are driving by the doughnut shop. And guess what will happen when you get accustomed to using your sword? It will be there ready to defeat the Enemy when you face a much bigger battle to compromise your spiritual commitment.

A friend told me about a childhood experience that shows how the *rhema* can be used to keep us out of useless battles. When he was in the fifth grade another boy challenged him to a fight, and they agreed to meet on the way home.

But just as the two were squaring off on the sidewalk, my friend's little brother ran up to him and shouted, "Remember, Mom says if you get in a fight at school, you're going to get a whipping when you get home!"

Suddenly, my friend lost his will to fight. He wasn't sure he could whip the other boy anyway, and he didn't want to get whipped twice. So he just walked away. Now that rule about fighting had been in their family since before these two younger boys were born. It was the "Logos of Mother," if you will. But when little brother repeated that word on the sidewalk and kept his brother from a fight, he was using a "*rhema* from mama"!

JESUS USED THE WORD
TO DEFEAT THE DEVIL

Of course, the best example of someone using the sword of Spirit to slice up the devil was Jesus in His wilderness temptation (Matthew 4:1–11). We've been through this account before, but let me make a few important observations about what was going on here.

Don't Be Surprised by the Time of the Enemy's Attacks

The first thing I want to show you is at the end of Matthew 3, where Jesus was baptized by John the Baptist and God the Father declared, "This is My beloved Son, in whom I am well-pleased" (v. 17). In other words, Jesus was heading directly from a great spiritual victory into a great spiritual battle.

Don't be surprised if some of your hardest times of struggle and temptation come on the heels of some of your greatest victories. That's the nature of spiritual warfare. The devil knows that our human tendency is to lay down our sword, take off the armor, and put our feet up after we've been through a battle. But when we relax our guard we are most vulnerable to attack.

Here's another important principle of spiritual warfare and victory. Jesus was "led up by the Spirit into the wilderness to be tempted by the devil" (Matthew 4:1). The battle Jesus was about to face was God's perfect will for Him. And remember, Jesus also faced crushing agony and temptation in the Garden of Gethsemane when His human spirit wanted to avoid the pain and suffering of the cross (see Matthew 26:39).

Now if the perfect, sinless Son of God had to undergo the most severe kind of testing, what do you think we need to experience? We often think that if we were just better Christians, we wouldn't be facing all these battles. Nothing could be further from the truth. God allows the Enemy to attack us precisely so that we can learn to use the sword and armor He has provided us with. You'll never know that your weapons can stand the test until you're tested.

As I write this during the Iraq war, one of the recurring refrains we have been hearing from our troops is that even though the situation is dangerous, they are glad for the chance to do what they were trained to do. One man who served with the 761st tank battalion in World War II said he and his buddies chafed for almost two years, waiting to be given the chance to prove they could do the job.

Jesus' temptation not only came after a great victory (Mark 1:12 says the Spirit "immediately" sent Jesus into the wilderness), and was permitted and ordained of God, it also came when He was physically weak after fasting for forty days (see Matthew 4:2). But Jesus answered each of the devil's temptations with the sword of the Spirit, the *rhema* of God. "It is written," Jesus said three times (vv. 4, 7, 10), quoting Deuteronomy 8:3; 6:16; and 6:13.

Jesus Knew Where to Get the Word He Needed

Let's develop the first of these scenarios to see how the Master used His sword to counter a specific attack in face-to-face spiritual combat and emerge victorious. The devil tempted Jesus to meet His legitimate need for food by making stones from bread—but at the devil's will and command, not God's.

Here is the full text of Deuteronomy 8:3, the verse Jesus drew on to deliver His precision blow to Satan. Moses said, "[God] humbled you and let you be hungry, and fed you with manna which you did not know, nor did your fathers know, that He might make you understand that man does not live by bread alone, but man lives by everything that proceeds out of the mouth of God."

Jesus did not pull out a random verse and swing it at the devil. In fact, His use of Deuteronomy 8:3 was so precise that He only quoted to the devil the part of the verse He needed. The Lord cut right to the heart of the issue. He was hungry, so He drew on a scriptural occasion when the Israelites in the wilderness were hungry and cried out to God. He answered by raining down white flakes the people had never seen before. So they asked, "What is it?" which is exactly what the Hebrew expression transliterated as "manna" means.

Now why would God give His people a food called "What is it?" Because every time they said it, they were reminded that the answer to the question from God was, "This is My supernatural provision to meet your legitimate need for food in a legitimate way, which is in My time and My way, not anyone else's."

God knew the people were hungry and needed to eat. But He wanted them to understand that how and where they got their food was more important than the fact that they had food to eat. And God drove the lesson home in another way, because any Israelite who disobeyed Him and tried to collect more than one day's supply of manna found it spoiled.

Jesus knew that it was His Father's will for Him to fast for forty days to the point that He was really hungry, and He also knew that when His Father was ready, He would feed His Son. Satan tried to short-circuit that connection, but Jesus sliced the devil's argument to ribbons by saying He would eat only when God said it was time.

This same principle of Jesus' reliance on God's power and His refusal to act independently of His Father runs through the other two temptations He faced. The devil offered Jesus instant recognition and fame by jumping off the pinnacle of the temple in

Jerusalem, because the devil had read the Bible and knew that God had promised to protect His Son. Satan even quoted Psalm 91:11–12 to prove his point—an attempt to use the *rhema* of God that was completely illegitimate. Then he showed Jesus the kingdoms of the world and offered them to the Lord in exchange for His worship.

But Jesus refused in each case, because He knew something we have to know too. Jesus knew that everything the devil offered Him was going to be His already in the will of God. Here's the principle: The victories and blessings God has for you are yours, and nobody can take them away from you if you will pursue them in His will and way. Satan can't offer you anything good that God can't give you if it is in His perfect will and pleasure to give it to you.

What about the things Satan offers you that look awfully good, but which you would have to violate God's Word to get? No matter how much momentary pleasure these things may bring you, they will turn on you and slice your soul up someday. That's why you need to have the *rhema* of the Spirit at your disposal to defeat these temptations.

Now if Jesus, the author of God's Word, needed to use that Word to defeat Satan, how much more do we need to use it? Every time we say, "Well I think . . . ," the devil says, "Gotcha!" All Jesus did was quote the Bible.

God Will Show Up when You Use His Word

What happened when Jesus had defeated Satan? "Then the devil left Him; and behold, angels came and began to minister to Him" (Matthew 4:11). That's exciting, but I have a question: Where had those angels been, and why did they show up after the battle was over? Because sometimes God wants us to be alone with His Word, that we might learn to trust what He said and learn how powerful and sufficient His Word actually is.

God is asking us, "Do you really believe My Word? I know you are hungry. I know the answer to your prayer is taking a long time to come. I know Satan is offering you something that looks good. But will you trust My Word?"

Would you like to have Satan leave you alone for a while and have angels minister to you? Then use God's Word to send him packing. Satan cannot stand the Word of God. He isn't afraid of you or your words, but the sword of the Spirit will cut him up so badly he can't take it anymore.

The angels ministered to Jesus' needs. He was hungry and exhausted, so He needed food and rest. The angels came, but not until Jesus had demonstrated that He lived by every Word that proceeds from God's mouth. In other words, God held off the angels until He saw trust being placed in His Word.

You may be wondering where the angels are with your victory. Don't worry, they're out there. God has a spiritual support system waiting to go into action that can do powerful things beyond your wildest ability to conceive of (see Ephesians 3:20–21—and sharpen your rhema by memorizing it!). But if Matthew 4 teaches us anything, it teaches us that God's power is released by our willingness to use His Word and defeat the devil in real combat.

If you want the power of God's transforming Word to transform you, and you want it more than you want to mess around with the devil and his toys, then take your Bible off the desk or coffee table and start hiding it your heart. God's Word is sufficient for anything you will encounter this side of heaven!

CONCLUSION

My wife asked me to go to a well-known supercenter one Saturday to pick up some things for her. I dislike shopping intensely, so I figured I would go early in the morning so I could be the first one in and the first one out.

But when I got there, the place was already packed with people because, unbeknownst to me, the store was having a huge sale. All these people had showed up to get their goods at reduced prices. As I stood in a long line with my few items, it dawned on me that what I was seeing in this store in relation to merchandise is the same thing that is happening in our culture.

Lots of folk will show up for a God who is "on sale," being interested in Him if they can get His benefits at a reduced price. But once people find out they have to pay the full price for the true God, they don't want to shop at that church anymore.

In fact, many people do with God what they do with merchandise at a store. They ask if something they want is on sale, and when they find out it's not, they put it back and say, "I'm not paying full price for that." False religion and human opinion always wants a discount god with few demands and lots of goodies. While it may not deny God, it diminishes Him so that His person and revelation no longer seem to have any transforming power.

Our situation reminds me of the dilemma that Elisha and his apprentice prophets faced when one of them accidentally poisoned their stew one night with some wild gourds, a cucumber-type plant with poisonous pulp:

> When Elisha returned to Gilgal, there was a famine in the land. As the sons of the prophets were sitting before him, he said to his servant, "Put on the large pot and boil stew for the sons of the prophets." Then one went out into the field to gather herbs, and found a wild vine and gathered from it his lap full of wild gourds, and came and sliced them into the pot of stew, for they did not know what they were. So they poured it out for the men to eat. And as they were eating of the stew, they cried out and said, "O man of God, there is death in the pot." And they were unable to eat. But [Elisha] said, "Now bring meal." He threw it into the pot and said, "Pour it out for the people that they may eat." Then there was no harm in the pot. (2 Kings 4:38–41)

This is a fascinating story with a great lesson to teach us. Famines in ancient Israel were God's way of calling attention to the insufficiency of the idols His people had turned to in order to meet the needs in their lives. When Israel went chasing after one of the false gods from the surrounding nations, it wasn't simply because they were tired of Jehovah and wanted a new god. They were usually looking to this false god to meet a need that they didn't think the true God could or would meet to their liking. So Israel poisoned the truth of God with the "wild gourds" of false religion and human opinion and unworthy notions about God.

There were a lot of these prophets, they were hungry, and food was scarce. So Elisha couldn't just toss out the whole pot. But they couldn't eat it the way it was, either, since it was making them sick. Something had to be done to counteract the poison.

What happened at Gilgal is a physical illustration of a spiritual problem that's prevalent today. People try to mix up the true meal that has been provided by God, which in the analogy is His holy Word, with the poison gourds of human thinking to make it taste better and go down easier. This man who threw in the poisonous gourds wanted to give the meal a little more pizzazz because he evidently thought it was going to be a little too bland and unexciting without his help.

But whenever you mix anything else with the all-sufficient Word of God, it actually makes people worse instead of better, because God will not bless His Word when it's been mixed with the wild gourds of human opinion and false religion.

The Bible doesn't need your help or mine. Ezekiel said it was as sweet as honey (see Ezekiel 3:3). You don't need false ideas or man-made rules to help you to accomplish what God's Word is already perfectly adequate to do, which is nourish people into full spiritual maturity. Whether it is the wild gourds of legalism, traditions, secular psychology, prosperity theology, emotionalism, entertainment, or any one of a myriad of man-made approaches to spiritual maturity, the result is the same—spiritual sickness.

Elisha resolved the problem of the poison stew by adding more good meal, which is the pure Word of God. He did not counteract the bad by throwing out the good too. He just added more of the good substance until it neutralized the bad and people were able to eat a solid meal. When we return to the solid, sufficient truths of God's Word, they will override the poisonous gourds of false religion and human opinion that are keeping us sick.

If you keep feeding on the truth of God's Word long enough, it will return you to good spiritual health. The Bible has everything you need to be all that God desires you to be. This is what God is saying to us about His all-sufficient Word. Are you searching for victory, deliverance, or peace? It's in the Word. Do you want to change the way you live or rescue your marriage? It's all in there.

May God help you to see that all you will ever need for life has already been mixed into Scripture. This means you don't need to toss in any "wild gourds" of false religion and human opinion, which only make and keep you spiritually sick. Stay with the transforming Word of God—because it's all in there!

SUBJECT INDEX

SCRIPTURE INDEX

The Understanding God Series

Totally Saved
*Understanding, Experiencing and
Enjoying the Greatness of Your Salvation*

Tony Evans explores justification, propitiation, redemption, reconciliation, forgiveness, and other biblical truths.

ISBN: 0-8024-6824-1

Our God Is Awesome
Encountering the Greatness of Our God

*Tony Evans has done a masterful job of unfolding the rich truth about
God . He writes with uncommon clarity, accuracy and warmth. A
treasured resource for all who desire to know God better.*
– John MacArthur, Pastor, Grace Community Church of the Valley.

ISBN: 0-8024-4850-X

Returning To Your First Love
Putting God Back in First Place

*Tony Evans has done to us all a service in focusing the biblical spotlight on the absolute necessity of keeping our love of Christ as the
central passion of our hearts.*
– Charles Stanley, Pastor, First Baptist Church in Atlanta, Author

ISBN: 0-8024-4851-8

The Promise
Experiencing God's Greatest Gift—The Holy Spirit

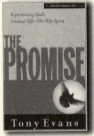

*Here is a book that points us to the Spirit's way to purity and power.
Every chapter is appropriately titled "Experiencing the Spirit's . . ."
May this work help all who read it to do so.*
– Dr. Charles Ryrie, Professor, Dallas Theological Seminary

ISBN: 0-8024-4852-6

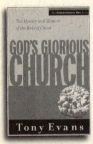

God's Glorious Church
The Mystery and Mission of the Body of Christ

Tony Evans shows how the church is nothing less than the ongoing
incarnation of Christ on earth—a living body with a mission,
a purpose, and an ultimate call to disciple the whole world.

ISBN: 0-8024-3951-9

Who Is This King of Glory?
Experiencing the Fullness of Christ's Work in Our Lives

In this practical, biblically-based volume, Tony Evans examines Jesus, "the greatest of all subjects," from three different perspectives: His uniqueness, His authority, and our appropriate response to Him.

ISBN: 0-8024-4854-2

The Battle Is the Lord's
Waging Victorious Spiritual Warfare

We're in a war, but Christ has given us the victory. In *The Battle Is the Lord's*, Tony Evans reveals Satan's strategies, teaches how you can fight back against the forces of darkness, and shows you how to find deliverance from the devil's snares.

ISBN: 0-8024-4855-0

The Best Is Yet to Come
Bible Prophecies Through the Ages

Tony Evans propels you past the hype and confusion of prophecy, straight to the Source. He skillfully unlocks the secrets of the prophetic program, simultaneously unveiling the future for all to read and understand.

ISBN: 0-8024-4856-9

What Matters Most
Four Absolute Necessities in Following Christ

God's goal for believers is that they become more like Christ. But what does that mean? In *What Matters Most*, Tony Evans explores the four essential elements of discipleship: worship, fellowship, education and outreach.

ISBN: 0-8024-4853-4

MOODY
PUBLISHERS

THE NAME YOU CAN TRUST.

www.MoodyPublishers.com

S<small>INCE</small> 1894, Moody Publishers has been dedicated to equip and motivate people to advance the cause of Christ by publishing evangelical Christian literature and other media for all ages, around the world. Because we are a ministry of the Moody Bible Institute of Chicago, a portion of the proceeds from the sale of this book go to train the next generation of Christian leaders.

If we may serve you in any way in your spiritual journey toward understanding Christ and the Christian life, please contact us at www.moodypublishers.com.

"All Scripture is God-breathed and is useful for teaching, rebuking, correcting and training in righteousness, so that the man of God may be thoroughly equipped for every good work."
—2 T<small>IMOTHY</small> *3:16, 17*

MOODY
PUBLISHERS

THE NAME YOU CAN TRUST®

THE TRANSFORMING WORD TEAM

ACQUIRING EDITOR
Greg Thornton

DEVELOPMENTAL EDITOR
Phil Rawley

COPY EDITOR
Cheryl Dunlop

BACK COVER COPY
Anne Perdicaris

COVER DESIGN
Smartt Guys

INTERIOR DESIGN
Ragont Design

PRINTING AND BINDING
Quebecor World Book Services

The typeface for the text of this book is
Berkeley